O'Mandingo!

O'Mandingo!
Before Mandela was Mandela

Eric Miyeni

Published by Jacana Media (Pty) Ltd in 2007
10 Orange Street
Sunnyside, 2092
Johannesburg
South Africa

1st Edition

ISBN 978-1-77009-345-4

Set in Sabon 12/16pt
Printed by Paarl Print
Job no. 000439

See a complete list of Jacana titles at www.jacana.co.za

For Njakeni, Thenjiwe, Errol, Rhulani,
Theron, Dumisani, Nkhensani and Isa

About the title *Before Mandela was Mandela*

Very few phrases are as colloquial to South Africa as the phrase 'I knew so and so before he was so and so'. By this phrase, South African black people are saying that they have known so and so for a very long time, meaning that they know so and so very, very well indeed. So if you were to say, 'Nobody can talk to so and so these days, he's a big shot now,' a South African who knows this so and so might pipe up and say, 'Well, I can talk to so and so any time. I knew so and so before he was so and so.' Saying I knew Mandela 'before Mandela was Mandela' simply suggests that I know Mandela very well.

The title *Before Mandela was Mandela* comes from a short story of the same title in this book. The short story tried to map out how Mandela would act after his release before he actually acted and largely got it right. It is as though when I wrote the short story in 1990 I knew Mandela incredibly well, hence the title. The reality, of course, is that I didn't know him that well then and I still don't today. I was merely writing a piece of fiction based on a fantasy future describing what I thought would happen around him after his release.

Contents

Introduction and thanks

All the pieces in this book were written before apartheid fell. What marks them apart from most of what I have written since 1994 is how abstract most of them are. You get the feeling that under apartheid one had to hide one's meaning and hope that it would still be discovered. One wanted to say it but one did not want to end up in jail, tortured or dead for doing so. In a way, this body of work is a lot more creative and bold. It is a lot angrier, too, because one was plowing through a time that was quite infuriating. Despite this, however, there is a lot more humour in the work. I hope you enjoy reading it.

It's been over twenty years since I wrote one of the pieces in this collection. 'Don't be used' was written when I was about nineteen. I'm now forty, fast approaching forty-one. My university student newspaper back then published an abridged version of the story. And I never passed Roman law, the very subject that sparked the piece's creation. In fact, after the second and last time I failed that subject, a certain Dr Lund, who was sitting in for the actual Roman law professor who was on sabbatical that year, told me that if the subject had been philosophy or English I would have passed with an A or A plus. Unfortunately, this was law and in law, 'We are sticklers for detail.' I think those were his exact words. At that very moment I decided never to practise law. I even considered dropping out of university completely until my mother talked me into at least finishing my junior degree and graduating. But I did ask myself what was the point of an examination if the examiner would fail you even though he could tell how well you understood the subject? I still wonder to this day if I wasn't failed because of the publication of 'Don't be used' in the university student paper. I hope not, but I would not be surprised if I was. The University of Natal in Pietermaritzburg (now the University of KZN) was so racist back then you could smell the hatred in the air.

The idea to publish this book, which you might say is a prequel to my first book, *O'Mandingo! The Only Black at a Dinner Party*, was born one day as I did some spring cleaning and discovered all these writings, most of which had never been published before. It dawned on me then that for some reason, even before *O'Mandingo!* (the e-zine that became my first book) was conceived, that I had always been preoccupied with observing life around me, writing down my insights and sharing them in order to try and improve the circumstances around me.

Some of what's in this book is quite surprising, even to me. A lot of it will take you back to an interesting time in our history. 'My life', for instance, took me back to a time when I absolutely loved Soweto. It is a tiny biographical piece that is in such stark contrast to 'Get the hell out of Soweto', a piece which was written over a decade later and published in *O'Mandingo! The Only Black at a Dinner Party*, that it left me a bit shocked by the radical change in thought. You might say, after reading both pieces, that Eric Miyeni loved Soweto during apartheid. After apartheid fell, however, he hated it. Could it be that I could not see Soweto properly until the barrier that is institutional racism had fallen? It is amazing what the passage of time can do to one's opinions.

'Before Mandela was Mandela' was written soon after Mandela was released. I am amazed by how accurately I predicted how he would act and how desperately I wanted him to work in that way. It is a naïve peace but it is utterly surprising in how closely it predicted the course Mandela would chart for South Africa.

There are dramatic monologues in this collection that were performed as one person plays, too. For 'Leilah' I want to thank Nan Hamilton, who is the only person to ever act that piece out in front of a live audience. We rehearsed it in her flat and I spent many nights writing and rewriting it to satisfy her high standards before she could commit to acting out the piece. Thank you, Nan. I don't think I would have written this piece half this well if it wasn't for you. I want to thank Sello Maake Ka Ncube for acting in the other dramatic piece in this collection, 'Like a fly on the wall'. It was through working with you that the piece got truly refined, Sello. To this day, I still find it an incredible experience to travel through the trapped mind that is depicted in that piece. It was a tough acting assignment and you did it so well, and with such generosity. Thank you.

The section entitled 'Love' is a series of three letters. The letters, which include 'On wishing you the very best', were never posted because I wrote them simply to view the love I was feeling inside myself in words. Collectively, these letters reside on the border between what is real and fantasy, because love has a way of distorting reality. However, one thing that remains consistently real in all these pieces of love is the intensity and the beauty of the love I felt when I wrote them. There is a tenderness there that I often miss when I observe how hard and unloving South Africa can be sometimes. 'Love' is no doubt my favourite section in this book.

Also included in this collection are my satirical pieces. These were verbally published by me as an actor, live, on stage in the form of one-man satirical shows like 'Twisted and vile' and 'Khazamula the nerd', which I took from Johannesburg to Grahamstown via Windhoek in Namibia to a tour of Holland that included Amsterdam and Utrecht, amongst other cities. For these I want to thank Peter Terry at The Windybrow. It is amazing to me that before our democracy was born a white man who took a chance on my angry, biting and often expletive-filled satirical comedy and launched my acting career in this country. Without this man, my acting career, as short as it was, would never have been launched and I would never have been famous in South Africa.

I have to wonder: if I were a complete unknown, would the first and only publisher I approached have published my first book? That publisher, Jacana Media, would of course argue that it published my book purely on merit and that famous or not, it would have published me because it believes that my writing is awesome, award-winning, brilliant, jaw-droppingly beautiful, marvellous, Shakespearean in its depth of human observation; a milestone of sorts. But I am not so sure that my fame had nothing to do with it. So, I thank you Peter Terry for inviting me to perform at The Windybrow's then

Potpourri Festival when you were the Assistant Artistic Director of the then Performing Arts Council of the Transvaal (PACT), and for finding the funds for me to perform at the Grahamstown Arts Festival thereafter. It is possible that I also owe part of my success as a writer to your creative foresight. Thank you.

Finally, I must thank Maggie Davey, Michael (Mike) Martin and the rest of the team at Jacana Media for taking a chance on my books and for being so enthusiastic about it all. Much love from me to you all.

Opinions

DON'T BE USED

Ladies and gentlemen, I want to come through to you today not as any party member, nor as any sharer of any political ideology. In fact, I must admit that I don't know much about those things. I want to reach out to you as a concerned student who has given some thoughts to the situation in our country and discovered something to share.

I was reading for a Roman law test the other day when I realized that the South African legal system is one of the most archaic systems in the world and one of the most chauvinistic. I was struck by the many cruel similarities between what the Romans did and what the Afrikaner ruling party is doing here in South Africa today.

The Romans, I discovered, were divided into two classes: the plebeians, who were the majority, and the minority patricians. The patricians were the rich guys. They controlled all matters of state. While on top, they structured the law to suit their greed. They divided the land so that the majority plebeians were congested in smaller areas while they, the patricians, enjoyed the rest of it. They went so far as to have laws prohibiting marriages between the two orders in order to make the plebeians remain too lowly born to partake in matters of governance and commerce.

We all know that South African law is based on Roman-Dutch law. The National Party, on attaining leadership in 1948, obviously saw the things described above as very important if it was to stay in power. So it instituted influx control laws to confine blacks (plebeians) to smaller areas of South Africa. It promulgated the Immorality Act into law to stop intermarriages between blacks and whites (patricians). So, it basically took the country back to Roman days. What the National Party failed to take into account was that these very same laws would create a resentment and spirit to fight the system amongst plebeians that would result in the victory of the plebeians after years of struggle.

Resentment and frustration born of these discriminatory laws has led to what is now a full-blown struggle for power between the races. Is it not clear then who is going to win? Winning means many things, depending on the opponent, mostly. Now, if it were a soccer game I would say you would be jeered at and scorned for playing so badly only to lose in the end. But we are talking war here, not sport. The consequences of a bad move can be calculated in loss of limbs, the command of one's senses and even lives, as the boys in the border war will testify. I appeal to you as students to view your position and take a stand on the winning side.

When I look around this conservative campus of ours, when I listen to right-wing students talk, I hear the voices and see the faces of people being used. You see, in South Africa, it doesn't matter what you think, really. What matters is what the government wants. I was watching the SABC television programme *Midweek* the other day, with the ex-news presenter John Bishop. I could sense from the beginning that the government was about to scrap the influx control laws. What hurt me, though, was the manner in which it was preparing the ground to make this happen through this programme. *Midweek* had this chap who was born and bred in South Africa – and was probably a very keen TV watcher, definitely a keen supporter of government policy – forced to stand up and argue against the scrapping of the influx control laws by echoing what the president of our country, what our prime minister, and the cabinet members of the day have always said to support the implementation of these draconian laws. Only this time, they made this poor man echo these arguments in a jungle of opposition. Not heated opposition, mind you, but simple, logical opposition that made him look like a real fool, a scapegoat for the cabinet members. He was being used. And I doubt that he even knew that this is what was happening. Why wasn't PW Botha put in this position? No. It must be clear to the public that he is not a fool even though he is a key member of the cabal that legislated what is today labelled as stupid.

This is also happening in the South African Defence Force (SADF). In it I see people being used for a purpose that no one is prepared to define in clear-cut terms. Imagine what happens to a nineteen year old with a conscience when he is told that there is a lot of unrest and chaos in a township and then instructed to shoot at a quietly mourning crowd at a funeral? We are talking torture, murder and untold suffering here. And on the poor recruit's side we are talking unequalled guilt. One may switch off and stop feeling at the point of execution. That's what soldiers do. But when one is alone at home remembering this theoretical zone of unrest, which ended in an unnecessary bloodbath, I can't help but believe that the guilt would be immensely painful to live with. And guilt about horrible deeds you cannot change must be the worst kind. By the way, while you are being tormented about what you just did – climbing on a boat without knowing its harrowing destination – your leader pretends that you are not there! He doesn't lose weight or gain more wrinkles. No. He is busy smiling buoyantly at a primary school to hopefully get more recruits for the future! At the end of this lies an overwhelming sense of betrayal for those currently working for this government. And, of course, there won't be any country to run to and vent one's deep sense of frustration turned anger. The SADF and the NP are sinking boats. Beware.

For those in the noble struggle, those on the all-embracing course based on the conviction that there can be justice in this land, lies brotherhood at the end. No betrayal, no sense of loss, only contentment and happiness.

I therefore appeal to you on this campus to show members of the black masses who are tortured and chained to the townships – the masses who see a white face as the symbol of pain and oppression, the masses who may fail to see you as a group not joined to this oppressive system – that they have support amongst you, so that when victory comes you may be seen as sons and daughters of Africa, too.

To do this is not as difficult as it may seem. First realize that black people are not hostile to whites who are for the struggle against oppression, that if there is a race for non-racism in this country it is the black race. Here's a small example: amongst blacks (excluding Inkatha, of course) van Zyl Slabbert is known as a white man in a black man's skin. That shows you the warm welcome that awaits you amongst the struggling masses of this country. Secondly, simply help in any way possible the SRC, Nusas and Azaso on this campus.

Join in and be strong because ahead of us lies a beautiful non-racial South Africa.

THE TRUE FACE OF CHANGE

I walk down the street in the middle of town and see a man of about thirty-four being whipped by what are known as taxi marshals for missing his shift. He did not arrive for his morning taxi-driving session so he gets whipped, publicly, at a taxi rank, in front of people three quarters his age. No suspension. No salary cut. He doesn't get fired. No questions. Just plain public whipping. Talk about rough justice in a free economy system.

Is this the change we have all been waiting for? I know that for a lot of white people this looks like change because in the past black-on-black violence was confined to the townships. But for me and a lot of other black people, it isn't. We've seen people bash each other up often, right through our lives. It's not pleasant but it is more like a permanent fixture of our existence. So permanent, in fact, that you'd be forgiven for thinking it is a black genetic trait. We have done it for so long in our frustration that some of us don't even know that there is an alternative to beating up a transgressor.

Alright, so maybe that's one tiny manifestation of social change – from the white side, anyway. But where's the rest of it? I mean, most of us know there's change, we feel it, we breathe it and some of us even choke on it. What does it matter if we can only see the major metamorphosis and fail to detect the subtle undertones? Isn't it safer to be blind, anyway? It's definitely more comfortable! But then again, what's new aside from Gorbachev's rebirth?

I think the most startling new thing is the unique nature of the vigorous change that we are experiencing in this, our beloved country. It's unique because it vibrates vigorously without being obviously visible. It makes a lot of us angry, so we take up arms now and say we will renounce violence later. It makes a lot of whites insecure so they emigrate to other countries and wake up missing the sun. It makes a lot of us blacks impatient, so we scream, 'More, more and more!' and do nothing for when 'more' does come. But this is also indicative of this change – blacks can now scream openly! It's just that the screams somehow seem to remain the same. So even here one detects only the symptoms. Let's try and find the soul of South Africa's change, then look at it squarely in the eye.

Attitudes have certainly changed amongst some whites, especially the girls. Years ago a white girl who was prepared to sleep with a black man was a rare breed – as rare as a virgin today. It was unthinkable! But not today! You see, there are many lefties today. Some of them sleep with black people to prove that they are not racist. Some of them do the same thing just to rebel against their conservative parents. And others do it because their friends do it. The reasons are endless. You find those who sleep with black people because they truly believe that they have found somebody wonderful to have a profound relationship with. Not all of them survive the traumas that come with sex across the colour line. That's another story, though.

Now, what rebellious, lefty, white teenager who detests her parents for being racists wants to be associated with racism? But she's still confused, so she reckons *what if he's right?* What if tomorrow he tells the whole lefty neighbourhood that her stance against her parents is superficial crap, what if all the blacks she knows start scorning her when she's trying so hard to be a thorough part of the struggle? *Surely if I sleep with him he will understand that I am not my parents? And I definitely won't feel so guilty once he understands. And surely his friends and everybody in my circle will see how dedicated I am through this. Surely my guilt will go. It has to go.* Give blacks what they want, she thinks, and centuries of debt simply vanish and you feel better afterwards.

But she wakes up the next morning to notice his brown teeth and the stale smell of marijuana in his mouth. He calls her 'baby', just like all chauvinists. And she knows about feminism because she studies at Wits. He demands more sex and keeps riding on her guilt-ridden soul to get it. He gives her a lot of the dope that she pays for; it's always floating around. But her guilt never goes away and maybe she learns that black genitals don't necessarily appease guilt. Maybe she realizes that some Rastas call lefties racist because it forces the lefty to prove that she's not. That it's a simple method to get into lefty pants; a Rasta joy ride.

So she feels all disillusioned for a while because this involves double trauma. Not only did she go directly against the norm, but she also got shortchanged in the process.

Why would a woman do this to herself? To answer that question maybe we should ask another: why confine yourself to the same old things when there's scope to broaden your horizons? Maybe somewhere in her soul our lefty knows that wisdom is the direct result of experience. All experience. Any experience. So she carries on with her rebellion against the rest of her kind. And then she meets another black guy. Ooh ... but this guy is so smooth. He dresses up and down and smiles like an angel! His skin is so beautiful! He scorns most things around him, including blacks and their attitudes. He hates racism. He sees no viable leader in the current political structure. He doesn't believe in roses and candlelit dinners but he loves her and wishes she could live down her past without guilt. He is so intelligent and confusing that she can't tell whether he is confused or trying to confuse the world, change it perhaps, mess it up, improve it? He drinks so much when he does, but he's so beautiful! He's great in bed, but God, he's so intense!

She runs away.

He makes her feel so worthless because she can't see the difference between his verbal intensity and general male abuse against women. She certainly can't trust him with her soul! But then who can she trust with her soul? What with the Rasta looming in the background of her conscience, her parents and their wish for her to get a good white husband who will support her financially in return for a few babies to carry the family name, her friends who are fighting the same battle and losing by the dozen?

It's all too traumatic.

So maybe our enlightened lefty feels alone and struggling to breathe from day to day. Drugs start to call in sexy tones and kinky sexual escapades look rosy to

24

her mind. But maybe she stays sane and feels that she's wiser for these experiences and therefore better off than her parents. Maybe she learns through these experiences that there are some black baddies and some black heroes and a lot of black people stuck right bang in the middle. Maybe she learns that we are people like any other. Maybe she learns that Verwoerd's policies were not exactly in her control, that it wasn't really her fault. That sex with black people isn't all that apartheid took away from black people, that maybe there are bigger issues at stake. That maybe her last black lover was struggling on the same voyage as hers. That his profundity and cynicism, like her own, make it hard for him to relate to life in this ill-adjusted country of ours. So maybe she wakes up to see the world from a more sober point of view.

And there you have it: another useful player is relegated to the sidelines because, in all honesty, sober points of view are not popular today. They will, in all likelihood, be popular in a South Africa that might take a millennium to create.

Right now, our poor lefty can't talk to daddy about all this because all daddy really understands is making money. And, by golly, how do you start telling daddy about a black friend, let alone a black lover? You will be disinherited and ostracized for sure! You will have no family! And who can carry themselves alone in this world? Mommy is daddy's double and whatever daddy says goes. That is if they are not divorced and mommy's too busy getting her own life in shape to be bothered. Anyway, she might just faint on you from pure disgust!

So real social change in this confusing country stays essentially hidden because it takes place within individuals who can't really talk about it for fear of being ostracized. To top it all, the change is in areas that are, in essence, taboo.

But what's taboo?

The Concise Oxford Dictionary defines it as a 'system or act of setting apart a person or thing as accursed or sacred'. Going by that definition alone, sex across the colour line is a taboo in both the black and the white communities. Whites are seen as near Godly by a lot of black people. And my kind and I are seen as near accursed by many white people. That's the sting of racism.

A black man takes his white girlfriend home. If his people don't treat her like a goddess he will field questions from black men wanting to know how they, too, can get to sleep with white women. This black man could be labelled a racist in reverse, a man who despises his own people and embraces the enemy, a ship in need of course correction. His girlfriend's character is never seen because in this confusion white is too dazzling a colour to see through.

I think real change, positive change, is invisible because often it takes shape in dimly lit streets and night-haunts. It takes its form within young, sex-hungry teenyboppers. It takes place between opportunist Rastas and guilt-ridden white girl-women. 'Ja, you won't go to bed with me because I'm black, you racist pig.' Ten years ago this Rasta boy could have been beaten to death for merely looking at a white girl. Escaping that and sleeping with her would have landed him a three-year sentence in prison. Today he can swear at a white girl in a pub full of white men and get away with it!

And so it goes on. Those who truly change become lost sons and daughters of Africa. Those amongst them who don't drink and spike themselves to death with drugs to stay alive, go back to the accepted norms to stay sane.

But true spirits stay on course and seek strength from within themselves because they grow to realize that the biggest struggle is lost and won within one's very soul.

MY LIFE

I was born in Soweto at Baragwanath Hospital. I actually don't remember a time when that hospital wasn't understaffed, overcrowded, or both at once. It has gotten worse over the years and yet miracles still happen there. You might remember that Baragwanath is the hospital where the Siamese twins Mpho and Mphonyana were separated. And in a sense, proper birth is a miracle there. How can it not be when people die in queues waiting to be attended to? So my coming to being was a miraculous occasion.

I left Baragwanath Hospital screaming like most babies, I am told. Other than that, I don't remember much of my first three to four years in this life. I am told that it was hard for my parents to find a house then, as you can imagine. The pass laws, which required every black South African to carry an identity book (a pass) at all times, were still a major part of the South African legal system. The pass shaped lives, ruined some and forced others to be over-determined to survive with or without it in the big city. My father spent some time in prison for 'pass offences' (being caught without a pass) before he eventually qualified for and was granted one and, with it, a house permit which allowed him to find a house for his family to live in. He and my mother were among the lucky few.

The house they got was a semi-detached three-roomed house in Meadowlands, one of the sections Soweto is divided into. I remember the address clearly: 901 B, Zone 5, Meadowlands. My brothers and I slept on sponge material laid out on the floor. There were weeks in which I only saw my father for a maximum of three to five seconds. The lounge, where us kids slept, had no door, and if I was lucky to be awake at 5 a.m. I would catch a glimpse of him passing the doorframe on his way to the railways where he worked as a ticket examiner. He'd be fixing his cap – part of his ticket examiner's uniform – and that would be the end of that for the week. Often, when he came back from work, we kids would be sleeping.

Our street was called Tshidzumba, a Venda name, because Meadowlands and especially Zone 5 was mainly a Tsonga and Venda area. That's how the National Party divided Soweto. There were Zulu sections, Sotho sections and so on and so forth. Even today there's a Zulu section in Diepkloof.

However, our street was somewhat of an exception. Our neighbours on the one side were Venda. I remember Sansan, their son. I remember many nights that we spent listening to him tell us about boarding school, the movies they watched there and, as he reached fifteen years or so of age, the girls.

On the other side we had Zulu neighbours. The women there found the idea of my mother, who is Xhosa, speaking to my brothers and I in Tsonga absolutely appalling and told my mother so. My mother made sure we never knew this and we kids got along perfectly fine, unaware that our parents differed to the point of disliking each other intensely at times. Beyond this neighbour's house was a Sotho family. My most vivid memory of that family is the snobbery. I also remember the man there winning the

'Pick Six' and collecting what was purported to be eleven thousand rands – a lot of money in those days – at the horse races. The man extended their house despite the fact that it was semi-detached to the Zulu neighbour's house. This was a very proud Sotho family. All the houses in our street were semi-detached but we still felt lucky to a certain degree. If you went farther into Zone 5 towards Zone 4, where the Tsonga school I went to was located, you passed whole streets of attached houses so that, except for the corner houses, you always had to pass through the house to get to the tiny backyard.

My memories of those early days in Soweto are some of the best I'll ever have. Staying out late at night was not allowed by any of the houses in our immediate vicinity. But we often sneaked out when there were visitors and hoped the folks missed us. Often they wouldn't call us back simply because there was no way we could sleep when the visitors were around. There was no space.

In winter we made *ithezi*, a fire made from paper, plastic bags, tyres and whatever else we could pick up that could burn. To be allowed to share the fire you had to bring any or a combination of the above ingredients to contribute. And, of course, the guys who started the fire had to like you. And, as is typical of most childhood situations, the bullies never contributed and they were never turned away. They were the ones to send us small ones to fetch more fire material. Around the fires would be the local glue-sniffing group. I remember 'Goofy'. From as far back as I remember those street fires, he sniffed glue. And I remember Tshepo. I think Tshepo was Goofy's sister's child. Ja, I think he was Goofy's nephew. Tshepo later sniffed glue as well. If you didn't sniff glue you were often getting enticed to try it and told about the wonderful highs you could experience from doing so. If you were not too well liked and your family was not too well respected, you were simply forced to try it. I never sniffed glue. One of the reasons was that I didn't stay late enough for the group to get too used to me. At about 8 p.m., at the latest, my mother would shriek out my name and I'd have to go indoors. Also, I wasn't one to follow the general trend. If too many people were into doing something, I would generally be put off by it. And, I guess I was well liked or else I had a family that was well respected because nobody ever forced me to sniff glue.

Those fires were, to a large degree, very central to my upbringing. That's where I saw people sinking into nothingness. That's where I observed tensions building up and sometimes ending with some boy being beaten up. That's where I learned a lot about people. That's where I learned to appreciate simple pleasures like good choral singing and the art of storytelling.

Around those fires, people related Terrence Hill and Bud Spencer cowboy bioscopes. They related Jackie Chan and Bruce Lee movies, complete with the soundtrack, sound effects, and made-up dialogue, as most of the narrators could not remember most of the English words they read or heard while watching the movies. But you still got very vivid depictions of how the movie started, what happened in the middle, and how it ended. You might not get the entire story, but you always felt like you had been to see the movie, too. It was great. And often, the evening would culminate in singing. We sang naughty songs like the one that went, 'Vagina get ready, the penis has arrived.' We also sang sad prison songs like, 'You who only arrived yesterday, don't cry, mommy's not here. Don't cry, you who only arrived in the big city yesterday.' But we were generally a happy bunch.

Early evenings were often spent playing hide and seek. I think some of us lost our virginity while playing that game. Saturday afternoons were spent challenging other streets to soccer games with balls made of plastic and paper stuffed together. The girls would challenge each other to singing competitions and *ibanti*, a game which is beautiful and a little complicated to explain. To play it you needed different size tins that you stacked up one on top of the other, a tennis ball, and a minimum of three players. It was a kiddies' game, and more specifically a girls' game, in which two players stood opposite each other bouncing the tennis ball as they threw it at each other past the player in the middle whose main focus was to avoid being hit by the ball. The players throwing the ball aimed to hit the player in the middle while trying not to hit the stack of tins which, if they fell, would allow the player in the middle to run from one thrower's position to the other's like they do in a game of cricket. The player in the middle would also attempt to take a few runs if one of the ball throwers missed the ball when it was thrown at her and it went far behind her. If the player in the middle got hit by the tennis ball, then she would take the place of one of the players throwing the tennis ball and thus the players would take turns to amass runs. The player with the highest number of runs at the end of the game won.

We had a glorious time back then. Some of the 'chayilenses' (a bastardization of the word 'challenges') ended in unfair play and we would finalize the competition with stone fights. I don't remember any horrible injuries

31

from that, though. It was all fun and incredibly exciting.

Soweto, even then, had its sick side. There was seldom a Saturday that passed without a stabbing taking place. One of the most vivid knife fights I also remember was between two women fighting over a drunken man. I remember going to school one winter morning and walking past a frozen corpse. The man's arms were locked in the Orlando Pirates soccer club sign, a cross formed using the bottom section of one's arms. That immediately told us he was a vicitim of the rival soccer club supporter conflicts that sporadically sprang up over weekends.

Even back then, we knew that you never messed with hostel dwellers. I remember a horde of them chasing a group of about five location dwellers once. One of the fleeing people fell and the hostel dwellers caught up with her. They beat her to a pulp with knobkerries. I still don't know if she lived to tell the tale. As kids, we were frightfully scared of Zulus in the hostels. We would laugh at their large ear piercings but never when they were looking. And we told countless jokes about them but never when they could hear us.

Soweto was divided. You were as stubborn as a Zulu or Xhosa. You were as black or as dirty or as stupid or as backward and uncivilized as a Tsonga or Venda. You were as sly as a Sotho woman and as materialistic as a Xhosa woman. There was social conflict but I remember everybody being somehow happy with everybody, ultimately. Most of the Zulus in my street ended up learning Tsonga from my brothers and I, and we learned their language from them. We went to different schools but after school we were neighbours and often lamented not being allowed to attend the same school.

1976 hit Soweto like an earthquake. I was ten and I didn't know exactly what was going on. I knew that the introduction of Afrikaans as a medium of instruction started it. But I didn't really understand what Bantu Biko stood for, although I remember feeling a lot of pain when he was killed in 1977. The hero to us then was Tsietsi Mashinini. We invented countless stories of that student leader's genius when it came to escaping from the police. We loved him.

My parents thought it best to send me away to study at Elim Higher Primary School in Northern Transvaal where my uncle was the principal. So I missed most of the excitement that came with the protest and turmoil that came with the historic student protests of 16 June 1976. In a way, I was lucky. But I was forced to lose touch with the Soweto I had loved. I went on to pass my matric and graduate from I.K. Nxumayo High School while my friends at home were dying or going to jail. I got my education – the little that Bantu Education provided – while Soweto burned, and went on to study law at the University of Natal in Pietermaritzburg.

I am both thankful for this and resentful. I can't bring myself to be happy with the fact that my parents had to do so much more to get what I have while parents in white suburbs just carried on like nothing was going on. I am resentful of the fact that ninety per cent of Soweto's people didn't have the option of an uncle who was a principal at a school somewhere or the luxury of having the option to send their kids to boarding school. I am resentful of the fact that Soweto has a lost generation. That thugs in Soweto have graduated from knife fights to gunfights. I am resentful of the fact that in Soweto today, a night in a shebeen could mean watching somebody blow somebody's brains out with a pistol. I am resentful of the jack rollers. I am resentful of the fact that black parents with money have to send their kids to white schools for 'proper education', a term that is completely wrong when one looks at the fact that very few if any of those kids speak a black language fluently. I am resentful of what apartheid has done to this country and to the people in Soweto.

When I eventually tried to settle in Soweto again I had been away for a total of thirteen years. I came back to stories of people being killed and robbed of their cars at traffic lights in the night. I came back to extremely quiet streets on summer nights. I came back to a scary and violent tension. I couldn't cope. I left Soweto and moved to town.

And for me the solution lies strongly in the hearts of the Soweto people. I see no outsider coming in and fixing things. When I was growing up in Soweto we knew of the tsotsis who lurked in street corners at night to rob and sometimes kill people. They would do this for a bit of time and then our elders would form vigilante groups and soon the crime wave would diminish. This is not ideal but it still represents the importance of taking charge and fixing things. We need that today, in bigger measures. We need to build our nation ourselves. There are no miracles that happen without human endeavour. And from the state, whoever that might be today and in the future, we need less negative interference.

I love Soweto and I always will. In that place were born some of the best people I know – gentle people, humble people, good people trying to get by. Even today, a stranger says hello to a stranger in Soweto. There's human contact. People still know how many kids live in which house down the street in Soweto. And they know their names, too. That's what we must preserve. That's what we must cherish and that's what must survive for all South Africans to know and learn from. We need love for one another as South Africans. We need determination. Places like Soweto are good examples of what it means to survive and conquer and chart one's own path.

SHOULD WE GIVE OUT MORE LIQUOR LICENCES?

There are many places that operate as night-haunts and sell liquor without liquor licences in this country. They are varied as well. Some are real roughneck territories, places where you could lose an eye for looking at somebody's girlfriend. Some are prostitute dens. Some are exciting and others are downright boring. Most of them get a run around with the police at one time or another. And often, with the help of some jealous night-haunt owner up the road, some close down. It must be a difficult job for the police to regulate the legal operation of all night-haunts. That's a given. The question, however, arises: Which of these places warrant survival? What criteria should the government use to give these places liquor licences and thus stop the police from interfering with them?

Let's visit one particular nightspot and see who goes there and what they do and, at the same time, let's compare it with other night-haunts on the same street. This particular place is of interest to me because the cops harassed the owner continuously. The place eventually closed down for reasons beyond those of mere police interference. But it stands out as a place whose police harassment was, to say the least, maybe not so warranted. But you be the judge. And if possible, answer the questions directed at the Minister of Law and Order at the end of this article.

As you walk into this place with me, you'll hear a buzz of voices. These days it's much emptier than it used to be in the mid-eighties when the manager then would get so happy there were plenty of customers, he would drink, get drunk, and throw a few hundred of his customers out! In those days, the place would turn a new leaf virtually every hour of the night. In the one hour there would be a live jazz guitarist giving a solo performance. Then they would show a Pink Floyd music video and break it with a Grace Jones one. Later, music would issue through a few powerful speakers, the pre-recorded music session would have begun and you'd hear Manu Dibango from West Africa, Prince from North America, The Genuines from southern Africa and Sting from the UK. The place was like one of the best television variety show specials I had ever seen.

Then you'd hear nothing but the buzz of voices. Some people would be trying to argue about the politics of this country – ah, the inexhaustible subject, South African politics. Others would be jeering at some artist for selling his soul and becoming too commercial. In those days, this place was known as a lefty hangout. That's where your aspirant musicians, moviemakers, fine artists, actors, novelists and poets used to hang out. And by the quiet corner, if you eavesdropped, you'd hear somebody saying, 'Come home with me tonight, you won't regret it.' Guarantees before sex. AIDS had just started rocking the world, but it wasn't a priority yet in southern Africa. Sex was cheap. All you needed was alcohol and gallantry.

If you crossed the room and moved to the backyard, you would find a fire burning. There would be people around it and stories would be circulating. Adults would be relating tales of loved ones gone by, putting their souls on the line – that's what talking to strangers about intimate subjects does to you, because you never know how they'll react, but this place had open-minded people. You could afford to be brave. Some people would be talking about the stubborn narrow-minded parent. Others would be extolling their new philosophies on life. Most of us who went there were, in simple terms, rebels. And we took nothing at face value. So we argued. You would see honesty at its most naked hour. Arguments and counselling would mingle and a friendly round would be offered now and again. We were the eighties' free spirits. We drank. And we ogled the women. And they ogled us. Oftentimes roles would be reversed. The women would pick the men up. And it didn't seem out of the ordinary. Chauvinists were few and far between. And once in a while someone from the outside would find all this too much to bear. Why are gays not thrown out of this place? Why are there this many blacks here? And from the old school, from among us regulars, someone would try to explain and a fight would start because men who despise those things that are different to what they consider to be the norm often seek to resolve arguments with their fists. The fight would end in one minute, give or take a few seconds. Fights went against everything we stood for at that place in those days. So they never lasted too long. After the fight, everybody would go on living. We would be happy that the imbalance was eliminated. It would be tranquil again until the owner got too happy and regulars would dive undercover again and support other venues on the same street.

But then where else do you find a freer flow from mind to mind on this Yeoville street? None of the other places has a fire in the open air. None has a bigger collection of people with artistic ambition. And none allows for freer debate without the threat of a knuckle fight, if not worse. None is equally quiet or has more variations in its approach to entertainment. So, slowly, we would flock back as the true faces of other venues started gnawing the sides of those of us who would, by then, be used to a life in the South Africa yet to be born. Those of us who, by then, would not be used to blacks being stabbed in the face for paying attention when some white woman comes over to speak to them. Those of us who couldn't bear to hear a venue owner tell a guy he had no right to intervene when some woman got molested by some man, that getting beaten up was what he deserved for involving himself in some other guy's domestic affair. We would flock back to see if our friends – whose addresses we didn't really know, whose last names we didn't really care about as we zoomed in on personalities – were back to anchor, as it were, their ships at this tranquil harbour.

And the tranquillity of a home away from home would set in. And the routine of humanitarian lessons taught through practice would begin and a few lifelong relationships would be born again. A few more hearts would be broken in love as people learned to accept and reject without prejudice.

We would flock back to what, at least to me, is the

closest South Africa has gone to having something as vibrant and family-like as the bistros George Orwell experienced in France and wrote about in his excellent *Down and Out in Paris and London*. Where you knew when somebody would start which argument at what time but never knew what reactions he would get this time around, where the patrons would sing 'Happy Birthday To You' to save the owner, happy or not, from a liquor bust. Where friends hugged, and lovers kissed. Where South Africa was represented in its entirety and there was no resentment for the other fellow.

Then out of the blue, a policeman would charge in and demand a liquor licence from the owner, and then confiscate all the liquor as though it had led to a few deaths by liquor vomit, plus a number of child abuse incidents plus a few overdose deaths and muggings, plus some pick pocketings, some knifing of individuals, rapes, racism, satanic incidents and general Sodom and Gomorrah!

That's when we would sit back and ask ourselves, 'What criteria do they use to give licences to sell liquor if the criteria isn't that the places help to enrich this country, like The Harbour Café did by bringing together people of the future, people who care not who your father is or what religion you belong to except as material for conversation as opposed to prejudice?' Why can't a 'harbour' like this be allowed to legally anchor ships of souls to enrich each other and grow around a simple mug of beer or a gin and tonic? Why can't these places be left alone when the worst of the lot go untouched?

Perhaps the Minister of Law and Order can explain this to us.

39

A LETTER TO THE WOMEN OF THE WORLD

'Men learn to love the person that they are attracted to and women become more and more attracted to the person that they love.'

Steven Soderbergh wrote that line for the movie 'Sex, Lies, and Videotape'. James Spader delivered it while Andie MacDowell responded with, 'That's beautiful, beautiful. I like that.'

Andie (who, by the way, I'm not on a first-name basis with) was echoing the sentiments of most women I know. On the other hand, most men would say that that very same line makes sense because for them, sex comes first, right?

What I like about that line is that it is one of the most apt definitions of the difference between males and females. What saddens me is that most women don't realize that if that sentence describes males and females well, then they, women, have the better approach in matters of love. So that what you find is a lot of women melting in the presence of hunks and letting them take the lead only to wake up to the realization that the man just wanted sex. It's a question of males and females working at cross-parallels for relationships.

When will this end?

This syndrome can only end when people learn to lay their cards face-up on the table and define honestly what they want in a relationship. When that is done they must toughen up and never settle for less, the idea being to get to know people well, first. If they are wonderful under those good looks, you will grow to love them, and if you love somebody, you grow more and more attracted to them. The more attracted you are to somebody, the better the sex. Sex, you see, should be the last thing on the agenda.

I guess what I'm saying – ironically, because I'm a man – is that (and I can't emphasize this enough) women generally have the better approach and that women should be leaders in this field, like they should be in most fields. Who would argue against the notion that caution is a far better approach in matters as seemingly dangerous as sex?

If it wasn't best to know people first before diving into a thorough emotional and sexual involvement with them, there would be very little argument against prostitution which, in essence, is cheap sex. But it must be noted also, that what works for prostitutes is that there is honesty in the relationship. Everybody involved knows what the deal is. So in that field very few hearts get broken.

My advice, if you don't need to know somebody intimately before you take advice from them, is that women should be stronger in their approach, they should compromise less and take time, a long time, before concluding that the deal was right for them in matters of love. This is because most men, at least most of those that I know, and I know a lot of them, will do anything for sex with a woman they find attractive. They will cheat and lie, they will act the gentleman when they are rogues, they will shower you with roses and champagne ... they will do all this just to get you in bed. And when that is achieved, they will be as confused as you about what to do next ... depending on how good you were in bed. If you were good and exciting you will end up being the only one confused. They will simply carry on getting laid with you and boasting to their best buddies about how good a find you were. If you look good, all the better. If you are lucky and you did not agree too quickly to sex and you like the guy, you might end up with a relationship.

Of course, women can do this too, but most don't. If they did, there would be no reason to write this article. Most women don't do what most men do because they want better intimacy. And that can only be applauded.

To women I say this: You generally have the better approach. Men won't give you the power to exercise this. But as they say in *The Godfather Part III*: 'Real power cannot be given. It must be taken.'

Fiction

BEFORE MANDELA WAS MANDELA

When he came out of prison he discovered that he had been dubbed the Messiah who would move South Africa across the tumultuous seas to freedom. He realized that, to a lot of people, he was God. But he knew also that to act like God when everybody already believed you were God could only help you quickly lose your Godly status. So, to the surprise of many, Mandela acted like any kind old man.

On the second day of his release from prison, Mandela walked unarmed and unescorted through the townships of strife-torn areas in Natal. He shook hands with residents. He sipped tea at a number of households. He talked to kids as if he were a lost grandfather just come home. He talked to them about school and about trust. He promised them that if they went back to study he, together with the other elders in the struggle for freedom, including Buthelezi, would secure the freedom for a long enough period for them to gain all the knowledge necessary for them to rule the country well when their turn came. He asked them to trust their elders in the knowledge that they were not alone any more. Mandela would often be seen patting a young man's back and saying: 'Young lion, with knowledge in your head, the world is an oyster, your oyster. Go get that knowledge.'

To the very little ones, he told tales of his own days as a child. It was said that at a number of houses he told the kids bedtime stories of the hare and the jackal and those of the lion and the hippo. He would at times be seen rocking a baby to sleep; rocking very gently indeed because he was an old man who couldn't afford to take too much physical strain. But it was still widely believed that his achievements at the time would be far more astounding for any man his age.

The first headline with a Mandela quote screamed 'ANC To Provide Funds Towards Building New Homes And Reconstructing Schools'. After every interview Mandela was heard to say: 'South African youth, go back to school.' Mandela was dubbed 'the wise old man' by the international press, which represented the elite, and by ordinary people on the ground. Crowds were heard to shout 'Baba Mandela' more than any other title. He was known as the father of the nation.

The response to Mandela's wise moves was simply mindblowing. Violence in Natal and most areas of the country stopped as the nation waited to see what the father would deliver. Kids went back to school by the hundreds of thousands. Debates on sanctions stopped for a while as money filled ANC coffers and was used to right the wrongs of apartheid. Extra beds were put in hospitals close to violence-stricken areas. Schools were rebuilt. Criminal rehabilitation centres were opened in most suburban areas of the country. De Klerk was forced to either back Mandela to show that he, de Klerk, was serious about change, or to go against Mandela and lose his credibility. He backed Mandela.

In his first year outside prison, Mandela taught South Africa and the rest of the world that people can differ and still work together for pragmatic and progressive change. He was respected and listened to by the PAC, Azapo, the NP, and the rest of the political groups which claimed to be working for change. Yet he never once called for any of them to work under the ANC banner. Thus, he deepened the importance of democracy.

It was a miracle to have a man of his calibre out in the streets of our beloved South Africa because, in all honesty, the only groups Mandela didn't touch and influence were the AWB and its affiliates. But even these groups knew that in the face of shining human compassion, no barbaric act could be effective. As long as Mandela was out preaching, they could never gain sweeping support. And thus there was the attempt on Mandela's life in October of 1990. But he survived the sniper's bullet. And his heart never stopped dripping love. He called on the kids, even at that grim hour, to forget about revenge and remember only the corrosive and self-destructive nature of hatred. The kids absolutely adored him and in the process they grew to become highly productive in their own right.

What could any South African say to this blessing of a man but thank you? It was only fitting that he would be awarded the Nobel Peace Prize in 1990, soon after recovering from his wounds. The world is simply blessed to have this son of Africa. We also thank the gods; for without this gift from them, this son of the soil, this humble leader of men and women, we would have known very little about what to prioritise in the struggle after liberation.

LIKE A FLY ON THE WALL

You come back home, open the door and you see space. Occupied. There's your favourite couch. The bulbs are exactly the colour you chose. You step inside, happy to be away from your desk. You feel a little dizzy. What freedom! Then you turn on the television. Terreblanche has a platform. So does Mandela. De Klerk stands between them. Will they blow him out and fight? You switch it off. The affair seems to take up more space than your hi-fi and TV, lounge suite and CDs. You feel claustrophobic. Dizzier. You drop off your briefcase. Turn on the radio.

The deejay rambles on, plays a song. You light a cigarette, torture the lungs a little while, maybe longer. Then the telephone rings. Shit! It's the girlfriend. She sounds scared. You answered the phone too jerkily. Can she talk? Yes, you say. She wants to know where she stands. She's tired of guessing. You pull at your cigarette. This time you bang your lungs really hard. Then you exhale and tell her to stand where she likes. She cries and says farewell.

You feel like a corpse going down six feet, being cremated, perhaps. Ja, you think, something died there. You loosen your tie and take off your shoes. You think back past the present to the future. All rather too quickly. Then you slouch on the couch feeling like a two-ton truck. You don't cry this time.

Madonna enraged the Papal throne with her show in Italy recently, the deejay says, what a woman. It's a pity she dwells in the past too much. I don't like her obsession with the dead. Marilyn is rotten by now, he continues. You smile a little and wonder if maybe you and Monroe are not the same. You feel soiled, so you drag yourself to

46

the bedroom and take off your clothes. You get under the shower and wonder if man was created to be an island.

You hear a knock on the door. Come in, you shout. Jacob walks in. You feel him take a beer out of the fridge. He tells you he's tired. He just pomped Mary and he wonders, giggling, if the result will be Jesus. He laughs at his own joke and tells you about Jane and Ashleigh. He doesn't know how to solve his obsession with Julia. Roberts? you ask. No, he says. He means the lefty at the harbour. You sigh and wonder what it takes to make friends talk interestingly about mundane things. Should I marry Rose? he asks. Would you like a cigarette? They are on the coffee table, you offer. Then you step out of the shower and smile. Jacob is part of the furniture but he talks, you know?

Bob Dylan comes through the airwaves and rips through 'Knocking on Heaven's Door'. This is another first in your life. Bob on a black radio station! Bob, knocking on heaven's door! Are you okay? Jacob asks. Yes, you say. I just feel so alone sometimes. Then all the sounds except Bob's voice and guitar and other instruments stop. It feels strange, you know? It's a funny version of Bob's voice.

Jacob breaks the pseudo-silence. I slapped Mary today, he says. I had to. These bitches don't understand any other language. You think about People Opposing Woman Abuse (POWA) and wonder if there isn't futility there. Jacob is a coy little man. He is harmless in appearance and tone of voice. He beats women up then sends them roses. And like a dove out of a magician's hat, they come back to him with tears of joy. Then the cycle begins again.

You feel sick inside. Your walls suddenly look like they've had a splash of shit everywhere because of this little man's presence. You can even smell the stench. You feel nauseous. You try to focus your brain so that you can stay in control. How the hell did you let this weasel into your life? How the devil can you flush him out? Your brain conjures up a visual of an axe lodged in Jacob's head with blood everywhere as you try and dislodge it to hit him again. You shake yourself loose and recalibrate your thoughts.

I told you to go to the Radio 702 Crisis Centre, you scream at him, with all the breath in your lungs. What for? he asks. It's not like I fuck my daughter or anything.

Jack walks in. He never knocks. Why did Jacob leave the door unlocked? Where's the party, gents? It's Tuesday, you fuckwit! So what? Oh fuck! Don't tell me you know this asshole! How are you, my china? he says to Jacob. In the brotherhood of men, you need not respect women to gain warm camaraderie.

You wonder if you shouldn't be dead. Then you ask if you can be excused. Where's Gina, Johnny? Jack asks. I just spoke to her on the phone, you answer. I think it's over. You don't fuck properly. That's your problem. They laugh.

The phone rings. Jo'burg Mortuary, Jack answers. You rush back in. It's your mother, Jack says. But why don't you ever phone, Johnny? We are all worried about you. Oh God. There we go again. You light another cigarette. You should take some acid, Jack whispers in your ear. Yes, mom. Okay, mom. Bye now. I'm okay, really. I'll let you know if things ... yes, mom. Bye now. Byeee. I'm putting the phone down now, mom. Byeee. Bye, now. Byeee.

Why don't all these people disappear?

You go to the toilet. If ever there was God-given

48

tranquillity, it is the solitary nature of the toilet experience. What a gift to mankind! Or is it womankind? Personkind? What a gift indeed.

Johnny!

What?

I'm going now, see you sometime soon, okay?

Okay.

Now how do you get rid of Jack? You prolong the tranquil toilet experience. You make it longer. And longer. Longer. You step out of the toilet. Jack's passed out on the couch, syringe in hand. He's bubbly and bouncy and yet so dependent on Wellcanol dissolved in water. You call the ambulance, as is the ritual.

This time he never wakes up.

The fuckwit came past your flat on the way to hell! You try to feel responsible, but fail. Why? You have your own journey, too. Then the pangs hit you. You could finish a whole goat. You make two sandwiches and eat. Traditional marriage without the violence suddenly appeals to you. Ready-made food. Kids to harass you whenever they choose and a doting wife. Childhood all over again. You think your dad was a lucky man. Then you drift away into sleep, ignoring the smell of death Jack just left behind. Will they suspect foul play? Are you off to court sometime soon? You dream of tyres, pangas and fires. You dream of blood and Count Dracula with a head shaped like South Africa. He catches you and as he sinks his teeth into your neck, you choke and wake up, perspiring and huffing and puffing.

You wonder if you are hearing a scream. It's the telephone. You pick it up and put it down. It rings again. You feel haunted. So you cover your ears and scream out loud. The telephone helps you along. Someone's being persistent. You run to your bedroom and bang the door shut, cover your ears again and throw yourself on the bed. The telephone follows you and enters your brain, screaming even louder. Then you remember. Off the hook, the telephone never screams. You tiptoe back in attack. You take it off the hook. As you try to put it back down you hear a faint, Daddy, daddy. It's your little son. Damn it, man! Trust this woman to blackmail me!

Yes, Lunga. Ku njani m'fana wa mina. The telephone wins again, strangles you by the neck and waits to see if you will survive the call. He wants ice cream. He wants to see your new car. He wants a bicycle. When are you coming to see him? Soon, Lunga, soon. Where's your mother? Now what's the problem, Ntombi? Why are you always on the defensive, Johnny? You must relax. This is a hello call. So what's up, huh? Nothing. Is everything okay, are you alright? You are not being suicidal now, are you? I'm going to put the phone down now. I'm tired. It hasn't been a good evening. Why? Did somebody die? Yes. Look I want to go to sleep now. You're joking, right? Ntombi, good night. Who is it this time? Jack. Oh God! Look, it had to happen sometime. But he was only ... bye, Ntombi. You put the phone down. Then you take it off the hook again. You marvel at the acuteness of your short-term memory. God! You remembered! Off the hook, telephones never scream.

You lie awake all night, scared that maybe this time Count South Africa will get your throat. Then the sun shines through again and you wonder when you fell asleep, how you escaped the fangs of the bloodsucker. You shower and dress up, tie and all, the regular yuppie.

You step into open air. Office life begins at eight.

You want to be head of the department. Then you remember the payment and price of dues. The boss wants this and that and you wonder when to lick ass, when to get tough. You wonder whether all this is necessary. The day rolls on. She puts a shit job on your desk. Then she comes back with that beguiling smile and shares snippets of the beauty in her life. She gives you temporary permission to live outside the office from inside the office through a window into her immaculate life. You feel confused, then a little happy. What an environment! Twenty million years or death it will take to climb up, but there couldn't be a better route past a shorter time. Here the telephone sings. It takes you to a concert of business melodies where you close deals and open new ones. You sell and smile, and then it's over. Slavery in the nineties. You wonder what you want in the corporate world. It robs you of three quarters of your life and maybe after ten years you will have a decent car and a house. For now you have an insurance policy waiting for your hair to thin out and fall off, for your spine to bend and your limbs to shiver holding off the inevitable buckling under your weight, for your skin to wrinkle and then to smile at you and give you peace of mind for the little of what remains of your toiling life. To give you money to travel, to live happily ever after, but after what, you ask. After what? Your sprinting brain cells slow down to a trot. You drove them too hard.

It all shows on the face. Are you okay, Johnny? You look haggard. Is something the matter? No, no, Sandy. It's just been a busy day, that's all. Talk to me about it, she says. It's been quite a day, for sure, she continues. I'll see you tomorrow then, she adds by way of saying farewell. Yes, see you then, you counter. You must see a doctor, you know. You can take tomorrow off if you want. You did good today. You deserve at least a short rest. Heh? I said you could take tomorrow off if you want. When did you drift away into her bosom? What for? Look, she says presently, forget it. By the way, well done on the Sun City affair. I couldn't have done it better myself. Thanks, Sandy. Wow, you say, the boss is happy.

How's Johnny?

Life rambles on. You step out of the office, inside your your company car you go, into the traffic. The Count's people are hooting and swearing, cutting each other off and rushing for amber coloured traffic lights. Taxis start and stop. You pass the taxi marshals swearing at somebody for picking up what appears to be his wife at the taxi rank. They take down his number plate. He must pay for stealing a customer.

You sigh and wonder what they mean by a new South Africa. Then you stop short of bumping the car in front of you. Jesus, you whisper, under your breath. Where did that come from? You proclaimed yourself an atheist long ago when people wanted your views on the Archbishop Desmond Tutu. Maybe the nature of religion leaves no holes for escape. Why did you whisper 'Jesus' in near crisis? Why do you continue to say 'Jesus'? Why can you not spit on the cross? Maybe it would be like claiming you never had a mother! Slavery, slavery, oh these bounds and barriers. Is it creative to kill? If they hadn't drummed 'Thou shalt not kill' into our heads, would we have a better society? How does it feel to create one's own atrocity? How does it feel to fuck a man who hates men by force, to

52

mutilate a human being, commit suicide? To say Mandela is rubbish when they all worship him. To make love to young comrades while your husband, their inspiration to keep on fighting for freedom, is on Robben Island. How does it feel to be the Pope and fuck the nuns?

This time you bump it hard. You kiss your steering wheel and draw blood from your bottom lip. It's a Jaguar. The woman comes out all apologetic. It's that kaffir, she says, no offence to you. He stepped into the road out of nowhere! I had to break hard. She doesn't want the police involved. She's in a hurry to some dinner somewhere. Will five thousand rand be enough? I have to go. Here. She hands you a cheque for ten thousand rand.

So many things happen so quickly in the city these days. Are farm workers happier people? Life is so slow there. You get up, pick the tomatoes, depending on the season and type of farm. The farmers beat to death those who kill their pets and steal from them. They call you 'kaffir' but it feels natural to say 'ja, baas'. They pay you with a bag of mieliemeal or portion of wine, sometimes. In the dark they fuck your daughter but it all happens so slowly, and before you even realize what just happened your daughter is old enough to work in their kitchen and you wake up to follow the sun. Is that not a happier life? Is it not a more tranquil existence? Is it not more rewarding to live day by day and wake up to see your son driving the tractor and acting baas when Baas Koos is away?

Then you drive into Hillbrow on your way past your Three Sisters restaurant home. You sit outside and order a coffee. Where's life? What happened to breathing? Then she walks in, all sex and brain, you think, and you want to lose yourself between her thighs and never be found. You get up and follow her to her table. You ask her if she'd like to order. Yes, she says. One coffee and a chocolate crêpe, please. You smile, turn around, order, pay and wait. You take the order to her table. You watch her eat and ask her if everything is okay. Yes, she says, thanks. You sit down and ask if you'd make a good waiter. Does she own a restaurant? No, she doesn't but yes, from the little she's seen, you'd make a good waiter. When did you start working here? She's never seen you before. Oh, no, you say, I don't work here. You just felt like talking while offering a service to a stranger. She smiles and flashes her wedding ring. What's your name? she asks. Johnny, Johnny Maluleke. You ask when she is getting divorced. Oh, this! Hah, hah, hah, hah! No, no, no. I'm not married. Maybe you want to know when I'll be breaking off the engagement. Yes? Yes. Tomorrow, she says. Or maybe never. But it's been a month and the ring is already feeling too heavy on the finger. I don't know if I can carry it for the rest of my life. I can help you take it off if you want. Where's your place? she asks rather abruptly. I'd like to come over if you don't mind. I swear I'm not a vampire. Come. Let's see what kind of hovel you hide in. Come. She gets up to leave then remembers. How much will this come to? she asks. Do you know? Yes, exactly ten rand and fifty-five cents including a tip. It's all taken care of, you say. You walk out and heads turn.

You get to your place and within the hour you are trying to make another baby. Whatever happened to avoiding dripping sperm cells by wearing Durex condoms? Whatever happened to the HIV/AIDS scare? Will God ever come up with a more innovative way to eliminate human beings? One sex adventure and you just waste away slowly. You shiver slightly and look into her eyes. Sex, they say. More. After a little while her mouth says, you are so good, your place is so nice, fuck me some more. No, she changes her mind. Do you write at all? Are you an artist? Why do you look so tormented? Sometimes. Nothing serious, you answer one of the barrages of questions. You should do more art, she says, you're too tense, too ... you need an outlet. I just found one, you say. That was an inlet, remember, you let things into me, okay? Fuck me some more. She's changed her mind again.

You drift away into sleep as time stands still. You dream of Mandela kissing Tante Elize and wishing her happy birthday. You dream of Jani fucking Terreblanche on a tombstone and drawing a love pact on a slab nearby. Then you wake up to find only her fragrance. She knew your name. You only know one of her innermost desires, if that's what that was. You drift in and out of sleep now. Time starts flying again. Not that long ago time tiptoed past your room. Slowly. Now it sprints by with thoughts of her rushing through your mind with it. She had angel eyes and a bosom beyond your boss's in beauty. God-given. Well carved. She was sensitive. Intuitive. Intelligent. Beautiful. Brave. Somehow you knew a Jacob would hit this woman only once and be worse off than scum in her eyes. You knew she would make him suffer for it. You knew she was worth a lot more than a bunch of roses. She was a woman rebellious but in full control and in love with her femininity. You knew that she made love out of desire, not submission or sacrifice. She would regret very little in her life because she dwelled little in yesterday. She would always be illusive because of her constant surge forward.

You slap yourself across the face. What happened there? you ask yourself. You saw a woman only once and now she's like clay in your hands. You mould and sculpt a supposed masterpiece. Why do you constantly do that? Is there too little that satisfies in this life or are you too blind to see with your physical eye? Why do you rely so much on your mind's eye? Are people truly mediocre? Is it more natural to be mediocre or do people choose it because it's easier? Is it better to wait for death or braver and better to choose when and where and then take your own life? Do we need the euphoria of war and the blindness of mass action to get suicidal? Why did you risk AIDS with a stranger, damn it?

It's eleven at night! You get up and look down. He dangles. JimJack dangles. Like most men you have a pet name for your penis. You wonder what sets you apart. You still hide behind a pet name to avoid reality. You still go wild at the idea of good sex. You eat and shit. Without oxygen, you die. So what's special about any one man or woman in this life? Would it be a joy to float on a cloud, sexless and free like an angel, if those exist? But humans do that, you remember! In its mind, personkind can be God! It can be a hobo! In its mind, personkind can kill, and bring the dead back to life! But every person can do that. So what's so special about Johnny Maluleke? What differentiates the farmworker from the astronaut if they both love what they do?

You take a shower out of habit. Sex is dirty. This was drummed into your head at about the same time as 'Thou shalt not kill'. You note that they might have been right on this score. Sperm cells are not the cleanest looking when dry and desperately clinging on to a penis

56

after sex. You wonder, though, if people haven't mixed up the physical dirtiness with the conceptual cleanliness because, you realise, in your opinion, the concept of sex, the merging of souls in an act that climaxes in a state of no control, a state of pure abandonment of the mental mechanism, is essentially a clean beauty to endure. In your perception, the state of climaxing is, no doubt, clean of all environmental and moral pollution. So sex to you, if indulged in with a pure conscience, can only be guided by the angels, if those exist.

You yearn after the nameless dame. You wonder again if she brought death past your doorstep into your bed to you. You wonder if she will come knocking on your door sometime soon. You look at the painting on your wall. Is it a drawing? The men stare down at you. They stare at you with tormented eyes as if paralyzed by learned helplessness. You wonder what drew you to that piece of art. Is there a part of you reflected in those eyes? Have we hit the wall so many times that we find it too thick to conquer?

Hush, you tell yourself. You could get killed for that. Nobody but a racist says to look at the rest of Africa! This mess has nothing to do with Africans! It is the workings of the devilish West. But if we are so good as to acquire freedoms, why do we remain in bondage after wrenching away control for ourselves? Hush, you say to yourself and look around. Hush. Hush now. No patriot is supposed to say that like fools, even after freedom, we beg the West to help us stay alive and then choke on the accrued, unpayable debt. Hush! But we must …

Hush up!

We …

HUSH!

So you hush up at last. Some strains of thought can be carried so far and no farther. The place you live in is so ravaged with chains that you find it difficult to express freedom of thought in the privacy of your own brain! You censor your own thoughts because of images of crowds dancing at the stake as a supposed witch burns with a tyre around the neck in the nineties. You block your thoughts because you've read too many stories of people slipping on soap in prison shower rooms and cracking their skulls to death. Johnny Maluleke, you ask yourself, can there ever be freedom in a country with a colonial history?

You step out of the shower and walk to your bed. You fall face down with the towel around your waist. And like an instant death, a dreamless sleep takes over and shuts out your tormented existence at last. Another day went by and you did not commit suicide. Is this a triumph? Or is this the highest form of cowardice in the face of torment?

When you wake up in the morning to chase the dream that is comfortable retirement, you wonder if a bullet through your brain would not pass as a mercy killing.

THE LONELY ROAD OUT

Jackson passed away, they said. What they meant by this is that he died. Jackson died of AIDS. His family began to see his ending life as proof that God was dead, too. In his passage out they saw proof that on this earth we are all naked, uncovered, unprotected. His disease was like a blizzard attacking them unclothed in a desert on a scorching hot day. Their pain felt like the pure lashings of an angry mob against their bare flesh. It was palpable.

They stopped believing in God today. Jackson died. He died naked on the bare surface of a concrete floor somewhere in South Africa. And God lost his voice.

I looked at the chronological order of things that happened towards Jackson's death. He had wanted to be my lover for years and on my honour (as I perceived it then) I swore that his sexual preferences – though neither better nor worse – were nowhere similar to mine. We became very close friends as he devoured lover after lover, frustrated that his latest true love wouldn't, nay couldn't, give back his love as he would truly have wanted him to.

He died, this Jackson, and the world is a bit emptier now. When he was alive he didn't take up that much room. Jackson was a small man, short, with a tiny skeletal frame. No, AIDS didn't have that much to feast on there. But like all victims of this monster disease, he suffered much pain. He was tortured physically and ostracized socially. And worst of all, being the impatient man that he was, he suffered in the worst way the disease could make him suffer. He was taken apart slowly and forced to wait in pain for his death. Despite his impatience, Jackson, like most of us, had a voracious love for life. He loved food and parties. When he was happy he drank with the best of them and giggled drunk, stumbling home, lover at his side.

I didn't see much of him in his last days. He became shy, less of an extrovert and his topics, normally varied and many, were reduced to one. He couldn't stop talking about his infection. Naturally, I suppose, he became a bore, albeit a tormented bore, as his features slowly became contorted, each day making him resemble a corpse being devoured from the inside from head to toe.

Jackson died today. It doesn't seem that way, though, because his ship out of here was so slow that when it reached its destination the people around him had almost emptied their wells of tears. His funeral was held long before he stopped breathing. There was pain at the loss of his life but it was a resigned kind of pain, a 'there goes another one' kind of pain, a 'surely he's better off now' sort of pain, a 'it's long been coming, we're ready' kind of pain. It was a vaguely complacent kind of pain that accompanied Jackson's final passage out. It had, indeed, been long coming.

I did not go to his memorial service. I wanted to preserve my memories of him, unpolluted by the recollections others had of his life. At his funeral, I stood at the back of everybody at every step of the proceedings from his home to church, past the graveyard back to his home to wash my hands. I was almost the last to leave, too, leaving long after most of his mourners had been fed and gone on to other funerals and wakes.

Jackson is dead. My God, I find that excruciatingly painful to think and write about. So I'll stop.

There. It's done.

LEILAH
One

Look at me. Do you want to look again? Do it. Look. Look at me. Do you see anything different about me? I don't. But by the same token I do believe that I'm special. That's no contradiction. Have you ever heard the cliché 'Beauty radiates from within'? Well, it's true.

My name is Leilah.

I'm a fun-loving woman who was born in South

Africa. But for all I know, I could have been born in South America, I could have been born in Greenland, or Europe somewhere. I have black hair. But it could have been blonde or red. It is what it is but it could have been silky soft or curly black. I'm just another female person.

I was brought up in a home that was neither rich nor poor, though it could have been either of the two. I had both my parents until my mother died. I was fifteen. But even that could have turned out any other way. I have grown to accept what most of you would rather deny in the quest for better positions in life. I am as human as any two-legged mammal can be. Come to think of it, there are so many people who have had the same tribulations as me that it's tempting to seek comfort in that simple knowledge. I have decided not to do that because the number of people behind an ordeal does not necessarily justify its occurrence. That's why I believe that democracy is for the intelligent and wise.

Like I said, I'm a fun-loving woman. But for me, fun must be in the light of day. At night and in the dark, I am haunted by nightmares that haunt countless girls, girl-women, and women all over the world. And by that I don't mean mere chauvinism. I have burnt my bra, too, and I think the sexual revolution was awesome. What I mean is the degree to which that sickness, male dominance, can be stretched sometimes, oftentimes.

Not only must my fun be in the light of day, and it must be with people who do not in the least resemble my dad. My fun must be with strong people. Whenever I encounter weak people, people as weak as my dad, I just want to run a mile because as normal as my home was, I could never have survived it without strength. Saying one needs strength to survive a 'normal' household might sound strange, maybe, but it happens.

I was an only child. And, to the rest of the neighbourhood, a *spoiled* only child at that. I had as many different coloured panties as some boys on our street had marbles. That's a lot of panties. I had pink little dresses, powder blue ones, yellow ones, and the ones I grew to love above the rest: the red fiery ones. You see, I grew to love fantasizing about blood and watching it drip from certain people. I'm glad that remained in my fantasies, though. I had all sorts of dolls. I even had a range of Barbies in my collection. I had a little house, little stoves and pots. I could get lost in my own world for hours. I still do. And up until the third year of lower primary school I was the top student in my class and my teachers adored me.

So why do I find sex a bit dirty? My family didn't go to church, so I can't blame the priest. And why can't I stop being promiscuous? You know, I just shut off sometimes and before I know it, it's over and I'm guilt-ridden, feeling dirty, wanting to run as fast and far away as I possibly can. Why is that?

This is my story. It's not unique but it wouldn't be wrong to say it's taboo to tell it to strangers and even more taboo to tell it to family. Think of this as a therapy session. Be quiet. Ask no questions. Let's see if that will help me. I think it might.

Two
I'm a lot more relaxed these days. I used to scream out so loud I could hear my vocal chords straining not to snap. And then I would push the scream harder and farther and

lose my voice. I used to do that at the mere sound of something I didn't expect. I know this had to do with my father.

When you've had somebody rake your soul with spikes, when you've had somebody mould your life with slime and decorate it with rotten smells, when you've had somebody force you to laugh when all you wanted to do was scream and rock your body with sobs, when the most precious dream you have revolves around the painful, bloody death of somebody you should love, it's not easy to stay sane. It's not easy to be brave. It's not easy to keep away the fear.

For years after I left home I would enter my apartment through the back door. I would peep through the window to see if daddy hadn't broken in while I was out. I would quickly open that door, run in and lock it fast. I would stand sweating in the doorway and wonder what I would see if I put on the light. Oftentimes I would do everything in the dark: make coffee, sit on the couch, take a shower, fumble for a gown. I took solace in the dark. I thought if you can't see him, he can't do you any harm. I could never have fun in the dark but I could hide behind it to escape the demons in my mind.

I was a nervous wreck.

I started buying love when I was seven. And up to today, I still battle the impulse to give a man a blowjob when he says, 'I have a present for you.' From the age of seven, every present I received meant a sexual favour. I ended up functioning like a machine. A guy would say, 'Come a little closer' and I would caress his dick! I remember my first date. I shook and rattled like an old croaked-up car. I sweated so much you would have sworn I had been caught up in a storm. I must have looked so stupid when I smiled to say I was fine, my teeth rattling away throughout my grin. I didn't know how to respond to the guy. Was he my father? Was he different? Why had I come on this date? Would he beat me up if I didn't agree to sex? Even as I knew I needed to normalize my life, I was so confused and scared, I didn't know how to behave or what to do. And yet, later that night, in a little dark alley as he walked me home he said, 'I brought you something.' I didn't hesitate. I didn't think. I bent down, unzipped his pants …

I was fourteen and a master at oral sex. My date looked like he had seen three ghosts.

When I was seven daddy said, 'I have a box full of chocolates.' I jumped up and down trying to reach the box. 'Give it to me, daddy. Give it to me. Please, daddy. Please give it to me, please.'

'Why don't we play a little game?' he said, with that booming, deep voice.

I think of it now and I realize that the game started long before the formal proposal. I would be sitting on his knee and he would be moving me up and down like I was on a horse. Then he would press me hard against him. The first time it happened I screeched and asked what it was. He asked if I really wanted to know. Yes, I said. He said I wasn't old enough but that one day he would teach me, if I could keep a secret!

'Of course I can keep a secret, daddy!'

My curiosity soared. I nagged him. 'Daddy, am I not old enough yet?' I asked. One day he made me touch it from outside his pants. He said it was daddy's little boy and that one day the two of us would play together. He called the little boy Big Willie.

When the game started in earnest, I had to take Big Willie out and hold him between my little hands. I remember the heat. I thought after a while Big Willie would burn my fingers! Mommy would be out on some errand. If she didn't go of her own accord and daddy needed the space, he would make sure she had to go and do something outside the house. He would start a fight about there not being enough beer or something stupid like that and create such a hostile atmosphere that mother would offer to go get whatever it was that was supposedly in short supply at the time. And of course he would offer to babysit. In any case, he would say, this is why he loved her. He understood, he would add, that she had had me all week and that it can't be easy for her. Listening to him speak I remember thinking, 'Gee, I must be an exhausting child!' It got to a point where my mother would just say she was off to some relatives for the day or weekend to avoid these seemingly groundless fights.

So, most weekends were shared between me, daddy, and Big Willie. Then I was taught how to kiss Big Willie. One day Big Willie just threw up in my face! Daddy had his eyes shut. He was licking his lips, his muscles taut. It didn't feel right. I remember the smell and the stickiness, the sickening taste. Later, I had to lick Big Willie clean! Daddy said it was protein and very good for me. He said I should think of it as cheese. I asked about the colour and he boomed, 'Not all cheeses are the same colour!' Then added that the worse it tasted the better it was for my body. Soon after that he started thrusting between my tiny thighs. God! Half the time I couldn't even breathe properly. Big Willie would throw up and that voice would curtly command, 'Go clean yourself!' A present would magically appear under my pillow or behind the door. I would raise my eyes after licking Big Willie's vomit and a brand new Barbie doll would be staring down at me.

I was lured into that game only to come out on the other side feeling small, scared, fidgety and dirty. But I had no choice! Or did I? 'The lessons you will gain through this experience are invaluable, my sweetheart,' the monster's deep voice would assert. 'Don't tell your mother or anyone,' it said. 'This is our little secret,' I was told. 'If you tell anyone, we'll lose the magic.'

And there was magic. I would go down on that man and look up to see a box of chocolates, ready to be eaten. I would survive near death by suffocation and come back from the bathroom to find a new, pretty dress to wear on the bed. What magic! I was seven and this was fascinating.

Then I started feeling soiled. I started feeling like a little whore even though I didn't know what that was. So I started asking too many questions. That's when the beatings began. So I told him mother knew. I was lying. But the next day I heard him shouting at her, 'What have you been doing to Leilah? What's this thing about you touching her genitals? Are you sick, woman? If she's making it up, then you are doing a damn fine job of bringing her up!'

My mother pleaded that it was not true and that maybe they needed another child because only loneliness would make a child's imagination so twisted. I knew then that I was caught up in a deep hole with no chance of escape. By the time dad entered me, I would look in the mirror and see a face smeared with shit! I felt so messed up I could smell it! I would touch my clean face and literally feel the slime on it! I would walk out into the street and believe that everybody could tell that I fucked my own dad!

I don't believe I just said that: 'I fucked my own dad.' Wow! You see, I was once told that if you can voice it, it means you can face it. Maybe this means I'm finally ready to face my demons. You are the first and only one to witness this big breakthrough and I'm not ashamed. That's good, right? Let me take this time to thank God. Thank you, God, whoever you might be. Thank you for loving me. Thank you for guiding me along up to this point. Thank you for life. Thank you, God. Thank you.

Sorry. Where was I? Are you still interested? You can always just stop reading if you are not. I'll carry on. It's good for me to let it out. So I'll just carry on, okay?

To put it correctly though I would say, 'My own dad fucked me.' It is not the other way around. He fucked me and fucked me over. My mother decided it was better to act like nothing was happening. I mean, I must have told her three times! She said it was all in my head and that I should stop telling all these lies and imagining things. 'Oh dear,' she would say, 'you must have had a bad dream, sweetie. Here. Drink your milk, you'll feel better. And don't you dare go outside this house and repeat such terrible lies. Your daddy will be very upset with us. And what if he throws us out? Where will you get a daddy who does so many nice things for you? Now we don't want him screaming like he did the other day now, do we?'

To cause a war in a house is a lot of strain on a seven year old. And when you are seven you don't talk back to your parents. So I started believing her. Dad would be all over me and I would imagine I was in Disneyland riding rollercoasters. I would imagine I was in the land of movie stars and that one day I too would be one, worshipped all over the world. I flew to all sorts of places, skied in Switzerland, travelled on the Blue Train, flew on the Concorde, conquered Mount Everest. Oh, how I travelled in those dreams!

'What's wrong with you? Go clean yourself!'

You see, I would imagine that what dad did was a dream and that my dreams were the reality. I would walk around for hours after spending time in the bathroom. Oh, that bathroom. My solace. A place in which I could cry and let loose. A place whose walls I could punch to stay sane. And the mirror in the bathroom, from which a stranger would stare back at me with scum all over her face. The mirror was my torment; the mirror was my insanity. I would sit on the cistern and scrub my thighs until they were raw.

The bathroom: my invitation to the other life. The bathroom: my sorrow, my love, and my refugee camp, if only for a little while. The bathroom: my step back into sanity. I would sit in there and convince myself that it really didn't happen. Wouldn't you?

I guess you don't want any part of this, right? Who am I to impose? I can hear your brain working: 'Who's this bitch and who the fuck does she think she is?' You just want me to stop right here, don't you? Auschwitz never happened! Soweto is another planet! You are just like my mother!

I'm sorry. I didn't mean anything by that. I'm sorry.

Please forgive me, daddy. I didn't mean to tell on our little secret. Please forgive me. I promise it won't happen again. I promise, promise, promise, daddy. Please forgive me. No. No, daddy. Please. Please, don't hit me, daddy. Please, don't hit me! Please, daddy! Don't! *If you touch me one more time I swear I will kill you with my bare hands! I swear!*

All paedophiles are spineless pieces of shit, right? If I had done that earlier than I did he probably would have stopped abusing me earlier than he did, right? Maybe. Whatever. I only exploded at fifteen. Sometimes I think that was too late.

You know, puberty is a rough time for any kid. At puberty you start to realize that maybe you're not a puppet, that maybe the parents are not as God-like as they seem to be. You come to realize that maybe your existence is yours to shape. At puberty, you start to question family values. But it's all so confusing, because while you're busy dealing with the philosophical, your body starts dancing to it's own tune. Your boobs develop, you start menstruating. Just as you realize that maybe you need to take charge of your life, your body tells you that you have no control. For me, it was special in a way. All of a sudden dad's caresses made my mouth water. Suddenly, I started getting wet with sexual desire. And I had no control over it! It became so hard to hang on to Disneyland and Hollywood and the Swiss mountain slopes. I would try hanging onto Mickey Mouse and he would start slipping away into a blur and I would battle to get his face back in focus just so that I didn't feel my dad. I clenched my teeth, dug my nails into daddy's back and cried silently in desperation. And daddy, he just thought these were signs of my enjoyment. Puberty woke me up into the hell that is incest.

How could I exonerate myself? I got turned on in the

process! My guilt mounted each time my nipples rose. I started getting obsessed with keeping the whole thing a secret. Dad sensed this and turned it against me. He started threatening to tell people if I ever stopped coming when he called. My guilt and humiliation just grew. They followed me to the shops, the movies, and when I tried being a recluse they slept in my bed. And the screws tightened. I just wanted to die or kill something. I would close the bathroom door and bang my head against the wall until I collapsed. Finally, he slapped me across the face again for being late for the 'appointment', as he called it, and I exploded! I told him to *never* to touch me again.

My mother walked in on this and I think that's when it really dawned on her for the first time. I was fifteen. She committed suicide and left me a note. 'I'm very sorry, Leilah. Please forgive me. Your loving mother.'

It's a shame because she probably was loving but obviously too frail to handle my sorrows. I didn't realize it at the time. I used to fight with her about everything.

'The blue dress looks great on you.'

'What do you know?'

'Come on honey ...'

'Don't you "honey" me, I'm not your husband. Why don't you "honey" him?'

'He's you father, dear, now I know he's not perfect ...'

'I wish he was dead!'

'Now compose yourself, dear'.

'Don't you "dearie" me!'

'What's the matter honey, why don't you tell me?'

I could not believe it. How could I tell her? It was in my head! Didn't she remember? So we just fought. Well, I fought with her. She never fought back and it baffled me until I took a really good look at her. She was small and timid. All she wanted was a quiet home with a man to provide. Beyond that, well, it was just too much for her to ask.

I didn't cry at her funeral. I believed strongly in the existence of a better life beyond the horizon, above the clouds or deep underneath the ground. Mom would be okay. And I forgave her. She was the wrong person to have died, though. Dad just stood there with his expensive black business suit. I wished to have been God. I would have switched their positions, mother's and dad's. After that I would change myself and become Satan. Then I would personally roast my dad. Do it slowly. Take one toe at a time. Then I would pull each pubic hair, one at a time. I would make thin little slices of his penis.

When people heard my story, they'd say things like: 'Oh, no, you lie. How can you say that?' or 'Your dad! Give me a break!'

I was nineteen when I ventured to tell anyone again. After my mother's reaction dad's warnings sounded true. 'Nobody will believe you,' he used to say. 'If they do, then you and I, together, are going to jail. Do you want to go to jail, Leilah? It's dark and they beat you up and they never give you love. Not like I give you.'

'Do all the other daddies give their kids love the way you do to me, daddy?'

'Of course. It changes, but it's basically the same. Now come here. I bought you a new doll'.

It came up all the time. The police, jail, how no one would believe me, and the beatings. I was scared of my dad. And my mother? Well, she just made me believe him more. And there was my best friend at varsity. I overheard

71

her talking to her boyfriend, saying, 'You know Leilah used to fuck her own dad.' And they laughed.

I dropped out. How could I stay? How many more people had she told? Were they all laughing behind my back? I had visions of all the boys in the men's residence talking about me and how I fucked my dad, my being a whore. I could hear all the girls giggling. And, worse, the men made me feel like I was on the verge of being raped. I hated the way they looked at me. It made me feel like I was nothing but dirty sex on legs.

And then there was Joe. He didn't try to run, he didn't try to laugh it off. He tackled my problems head on. He was different. He once asked, 'If your mother died at the mere discovery of what happened to you, how did *you* survive?'

I couldn't answer at the time. But that set me on my path. I took stock of my strengths and I wrote this in my little book of thoughts:

To have a good mind is to know that you are here to survive. If you never strike chaos as a child, you stumble into walls as an adult, unless you die too early in life! Hardship is the biggest section of this life we live in. Unless we see ourselves as survivors, we are doomed to only live silly, wanton lives. Like I always say, becoming an adult is like buying a house. You find that it has a pantry, then decide if you need the pantry. If the answer is no, you decide what to do with the space. Maybe it's too small for a study. So you break down the wall and build it farther away. It takes energy and time. It takes patience and it takes money. But you'll be happier when it's done. The same goes for your personality. You inherit it, and then fix it.

Isn't that lovely? Oh, here's another entry:

There are those things you'll acquire as a foetus. These you very seldom can change. Make friends with them, no matter how ugly they are. They are most likely to be in your presence for as long as you live. Make friends with them, you will find that they quickly recede into the background, leaving you free to attend to growth in other important areas that can be changed for the better.

Then there are those things you acquire as a child. Some of these you demand but mostly they are forced on you. These you can discard if you please. They are essentially circumstantial. It will take time, because childhood can last a lifetime. It will take pain, because to change them you have to admit that you are not perfect. The key is to realize that you are not to blame for these imperfections. You have no reason to be guilt-ridden.

It will take intelligence, because knowing which of these things you root out need replacement, knowing how to go about doing these, all this takes a good mind. A good mind is simply having confidence in yourself. It will take patience because it takes time to undo what took time to build up. It will take guts because to change things you need to be a non-conformist. Otherwise accept everything about yourself and never apologise. Be happy with who you are.

I wish Joe was here. I couldn't say all this at the time. I couldn't find reasons for my behaviour. I would open

73

my legs here, open them there. I got my image so tangled up with daddy's that I couldn't see straight. I couldn't see how I could be something separate from the slime that he was. So I drank and spiked myself. When you are high the least of your concerns is reality. It's just that whenever I got back to earth, my attitude would envelope me again. The world owed me something! Somebody had robbed me of a childhood somewhere! And the whole world was involved! So I fought against everybody, everywhere, about everything. Everyone represented dad. Wherever I went, dad was there, stalking me like a ghost. That's how I lost my Joe. Two years! That's how long he stuck it out. Then he gave up. He said that if he did not leave me we would both sink and die.

One day it dawned on me: daddy wasn't me! He just used me when I was least powerful, least equipped to make decisions! And I woke up. It was like having a nightmare and waking up to a friendly smile, knowing that that smile had been trying to comfort you right through the nightmare. Daddy was dirty! I wasn't! I'm not dirty today, I never was and the future is mine to shape.

I am strong now, but I would never have done it alone. That's why I want to thank you. Every time somebody listens, I grow a little stronger.

My name is Leilah. I can't meet you in person even though I would really love to. But you have no idea how much you've given me. Daddy seems so far away right now. I mean, I left home when my mother died. I waitressed my way through everything I have. But I carried daddy with me. He'd pop up from behind the door, enter my dreams, jump me from behind! It was horrible. No matter how far I travelled, he'd be there, in my mind. But every time

I talk about it all he disappears more and more. It is so comforting.

I don't ask for much. All I want is a little peace, some kind of peace. I want to walk up to a mirror and be able to smile at myself. I want to walk away from that mirror and pat myself on the shoulder, feeling good with what I saw. I just want to sleep and not wake up screaming. I think it would be so nice, just so beautiful, to look forward to a new day with a smile on my face. That's all I want. I don't think that's so much to ask for, do you? And every time somebody sits back and listens without jumping in, and criticizing, you know, every time somebody listens, my dreams get sweeter and I sleep a little longer. That's why I want to thank you for reading this. It makes you a truly beautiful person. I wish there were more of you.

It does seem strange, doesn't it? Here's a woman who could have been Jane or Mary or Priscilla or Thembi. That's the chilling thing about my story. Should we let more people describe their lives this way? Should we have what happened to me happen to others? I find that difficult to answer. What I went through had certain benefits. I definitely don't revere men like most women do. So I'm the unlikeliest candidate for abuse. The way I feel about sex? Well, sex to me, to tell you the truth, isn't half as frightening or dirty or as big a taboo as it is to some women that I have met. Through my pain, I've learned to appreciate myself more because I've had to fight to believe that anything about me is great. It's hard to knock my confidence down, unlike some women I know. And that's not like having airs. I don't find other people's troubles trivial.

I don't look down on blacks or hate whites for being

white. Abuse taught me humility and a sense of what's human. It gave me love for fellow people and for life. I survived my abuse and like all horror survivors, it gave me strength. It built a person out of me. Very few problems seem insurmountable to me today. So in a twisted sort of way, I am thankful for my troubles.

Should kids be abused to gain strength of character? And if you believe, like I do, that the answer is *no*, then tell me, how should kids be brought up to be strong, to have character? I can't answer that for you now. All I can say is, open your ears and listen, because in South Africa we can heal a lot by simply tuning in to the screams around us. At most, it requires that we give our vocal chords a holiday.

Thank you for living in my world for these few pages. Much love.

Love

ON WISHING YOU THE VERY BEST

There's a most beautiful side to this place we live in. It is located two streets down from your block of flats towards Observatory.

I came back tired from work the other day and tried to sleep and failed. It was one of those very warm evenings that discourage staying indoors. So I decided to take a walk down Rocky Street. That always clears my mind – walking. It oils my creative machinery and makes me smile, feeling free. I just loosen up and throw one leg after the other under my weight and before I know it I'm sucking in the littlest of beauties around me.

As I neared the cut-off point where Rocky Street disappears into Observatory Road, my mind conjured up a chance meeting with you at the corner shop there. You would be standing facing one of the stands trying to decide which chocolate to buy. I would come from behind you and say, 'You must be working very hard, Julia.' You would turn around and I would say, 'How is it going?' You would then tell me and I would wish you the best and give you my contact number, asking you to call me when the heat was off. And of course, the meeting never took place. In fact, as I reached the shop, the owner was busy locking up.

I turned the corner, and as I went past your block, I tried to imagine which flat yours would be. I turned right into Frances Street and yes, that's when I discovered the beautiful side (at least by night) to this place we live in. I saw real estate with low walls and spacious gardens that seemed to force the houses to recede into the background in humble submission. I saw unoccupied patches of land with grass seemingly growing wild and unattended. I heard a screaming silence and felt the tranquillity of abandonment. It felt like the exact place to retire to after the bubbles and boils of this city.

I found myself walking like I would in a peaceful dream. The night was quite beautiful, there was something captivatingly luminous about the summer darkness. There was something very warm about the hesitantly cold air. It felt as though something would rush out of nowhere and create a stir then quietly recede into the night shadows. And me, I was just a passive recipient. My whole walk was instantly romanticized. I walked homeward feeling like a person being caressed gently down the back.

And here is where I'm going to tell you something that you probably don't want to hear. Here is where I blow my cool and tell you something that might push you away for good. But I'll tell you anyway because you deserve to know the gifts you pass on to others even if it is by accident.

I felt, after the walk, as connected as I felt after the time I spent with you on New Year's Day. I felt a peaceful kind of connection. I felt like a human being with no cares, no worries. Let me put it this way: you are the first person that I've made love to with my heart and soul. There's a beautiful tranquillity in that. This, however, does not spell out a contract for you. I just want you to know that without you, I would still be in the dark if somebody asked what it really meant to have a truly meaningful connection across the sex barrier. Today, it means climaxing by accident, not by design. It means losing yourself in the giving of yourself to the other without being aware of it. It means merging with the soul for the accidental fusion of the physical. It means being so thoroughly at peace that the only danger lies in being surrounded by people you shouldn't trust.

My friends know you as my Delilah because you make me feel like Samson at his weakest hour. I don't want to mould you, though. This gushing of emotion is not an attempt at emotional blackmail. You and I can just be friends and I'll be happy. I have written somewhere in my book of thoughts that I am so at peace with you that you could kill me and yet you could give me the brightest spark of life and I don't give a damn either way. It is enough to know that somewhere in this world is somebody with whom I have that kind of connection. This is not a game. You obviously don't know this, but I find social and sexual games rather tedious most of the time. I revel in what I call my naked hours, when I can bring out exactly what I feel for all to see. And the fact is that you can even ridicule all this and it still won't take from my experience. That's the plus that comes with honesty in the unveiling of emotions felt deep inside. I am writing this out of the selflessness I learned when I felt the connection with you.

You showed me the beauty of giving to those you feel for without insisting on emotional guarantees. So, even if it didn't happen for you, there is no bother for me. You could be my daughter, you could be my son, you could be my father, you could be a corpse, you could be a jailbird, you could be a junkie, or a criminal, or a priest, or a hosepipe, and I would still love you the same. This isn't about your physical attributes, it isn't about the way you talk and it isn't about your beliefs. It is about everything that makes up the Julia that gave me this sanity in this mad world, and I don't care what 'everything' is. You are okay in my mind and I like dealing with that.

Anyway, I reached this place, my rented place, after the walk and tried to recapture this whole experience for you because now and again you do cross my mind, dancing like the wind.

You must be working very hard, Julia. I wish you the very best. I feel sorry that I missed you on your birthday. I came rather late. I thought I saw you inside a Beetle near the corner shop on Rocky Street. But the person I saw had their back to me and I wasn't sure, so I walked on to Rumours. I hope that you had a truly happy birthday. And all the best with your dissertation.

Please forgive me if all of this is too much to bare. My name is Eric and I work in extremes. You had to get this back at the same velocity you gave it to me. I have been dying to at least let you know all this before you disappeared. It's probably a good thing that I took that walk and found a similar attachment to the beautiful side (at least by night) to this place we live in. It gave me the inspiration to spell these feelings out, for better or for worse. And for both our sakes, I hope it is for the better.

I am off to bed now. I hope to extend this walk I just completed in a sweet dream. Good night.

I NEARLY FELL IN LOVE AGAIN TONIGHT

I nearly fell in love again tonight. I remember looking at her and thinking, 'You remind me more of a doctor than a lawyer.' I don't know why she did or does. But maybe it doesn't matter anyway. Who knows what matters these days?

We danced again tonight. She singled me out from the crowd, or so it seemed to me at the time. And whenever I disappeared from the dance floor for a minute, she seemed to run around to simply locate where I was or to go deeper in to investigate what I might be doing.

I wasn't doing much. Talking to a male friend away from a female dancing companion who singled you out from the crowd to dance with you isn't much, now is it? She went back to the dance floor. I went back and joined her in the dance again. She didn't chase me away because maybe she does agree that talking to a male companion away from a female who singled you out from the crowd for a dance isn't much to worry about.

There really is something magical about Mike's parties, Nicky's music, and the whole atmosphere up on that hillock in Troyeville near the Bank of Lisbon in Johannesburg. And perhaps that's why perfectly sane friends of mine will take home confused gay boys who compromise themselves and take pussy when there is no perfectly shaped penis to suck. Perhaps that's why my perfectly sane friends, perfectly drugged out and inebriated friends, perfectly lonely friends, take home these perfectly confused gay boys and fuck them. Perhaps.

We danced again tonight. But I felt dirty, sweaty. I thought I had a bad smell. And her smile, glorious as it always is, couldn't make me think otherwise. So I leaned closer to her delicate face and said, 'I'm going to take a break from all this.' She smiled what seemed like a go-ahead. I left. You would think that this happened quickly. But it didn't because the decision before the action to pull my face away from hers was ever so slightly delayed so that when I did finally pull my face away, it made my whole exit seem a bit like an ill-fitting pair of men's underwear riding one bum on a clumsy early morning. Not smooth. I could almost see all of this reflected in her eyes. But I was in that mental state where I can never tell whether I'm drunk or tired and everything seems stuck in between spaces and never defined. I wasn't about to clean this exit up. I needed the break right then. And she wasn't invited.

I reached home and chatted to my lovely, curious, and altogether motherly flatmate with the golden singing voice that some pathology has stopped her from using and ran the bath. That done, I soaked myself in the hot water and read for the next hour. All the while I'm thinking about what I'm going to tell her once I get back to that party, once I've asked her to get away from it all for a while and catch some fresh air. This is what I'm going to say to her, 'From the moment I first ever saw your face, I fell in love with your eyes, your smile, that dark mane of hair. And since then I've always thought of you as the beautiful girl with the golden smile and the gorgeous eyes and it's been a battle to remember your name. It's terrible, I know, but could you forgive me first and then tell me your name again?' I couldn't even begin to imagine what her reaction would be, let alone whether I would even have the courage to speak when I saw her. But I dressed up nonetheless and prepared for my second entrance on that hillock where Mike's parties with Nicky's music always are. I arrived smelling clean and feeling all fresh and crisp again and was met by an empty dance floor packed full of people.

She had left.

I kept my cool and joined in the dancing, hoping that she would reappear from nowhere, seek me out again. She didn't. I danced on. Time ticked by. I offered an old friend and his two newly made buddies a ride to their respective homes. They were too drunk. They wanted to walk. But this 'we'll walk don't worry' line sounded like a group suicide threat. Was I drunk or had I sobered up? It didn't matter. She was gone, it seemed, and I had to do something to strangle time. Kill it while I waited, hoping.

Group suicide averted, I drove back to the party again and found an ex-girlfriend on the dance floor with a friend of mine. They had one slow dance after looking at me with an inexplicable unease, and then went home to fuck. I could see and smell it as if I was there, allowed to watch it live. I felt jealousy stab. I flinched. The lover I took, the same lover who took me for a while, too, also took me out of my horror dream-world by saying 'goodbye' and somehow making that sound like 'come with me'. She left.

My friend took home the drunk and confused gay boy who couldn't find a willing penis to suck. I watched yet another closet gay boy take home yet another pretty foreign girl who got herself addicted to South Africa. I watched a friend of mine, whose sexual identity seems mired in a cloud of deception and what appears to me to be denial, watch me. I wondered if he thought that I would fuck him, maybe tonight. So I put on my big 'I am a heterosexual' sign high up on my forehead and paraded it for him to see. I watched a straight friend of mine working his way to yet another possibility of rejection by yet another straight female. I looked around the dance floor and felt empty inside. I walked down the stairs, out the gate, and into my little car and drove straight home. On arrival I immediately thought of calling Nonkululeko in Kampala. Nonkululeko, my lover, my girlfriend, my friend, my love, my everything by satellite. I wanted to tell her, 'Nonkululeko, I'm alone and lonely. God, I feel so alone, Nkuli, it makes my bones ache.'

Then I looked at the time: ten minutes to four o'clock in the morning. No go. It was too early. I could not raise enough courage to jingle her awake. So I wrote this true story instead. I wrote it all down, you see, because I felt this need to say that I am at war with being alone. I am at war with loneliness. That I'm too filled up with you to have space for another woman who deserves my loyalty as much as you did when you were here and not in East Africa. You see, I wanted to say that somebody nearly rocked that secure, insecure place in me and I nearly fell in love again tonight. Amidst the drunkenness, the drugs, the promiscuity, the magic, the music, the laughter, the lust, the dancing, the perfect little tragedies. I nearly fell in love again tonight and then she disappeared.

But I felt alive again. I felt centred and from that centre I could read the terror intertwined in a dance with the horror that is the loneliness of the Yeovilite as is the custom to call most of us 'guests', at Mike's parties with Nicky's music. All of us (mostly Jo'burgers) who live or once lived in the suburb called Yeoville. Then I thought, God, the nineties are a cruel time, aren't they? You can't fuck with abandon because AIDS rules! You can't admit to wanting to be with others because you ought to be strong alone! You can't get married unless there's a big haul to be made at the centre of the marriage! If you just get married because it feels right to do it then you are just being all penis like your father before you, you are just being all vagina like your mother before you and nothing else. After all, you think, isn't marriage the elevation of sex organs to a platform of leadership? If it wasn't to make babies, why else would you marry? And who wants to become their parents in this time of heightened individual power and independence, anyway?

The horror of it!

God! We are so disconnected, so alone. But, as the advertisement says, in this pathetic state, we are the strongest we have ever been as a species. We embrace and hang on to that thought for dear life because those who put it on television made us forget that we need and have each other! Those who put it on television made us forget to remember that we are strong alone, yes, but that one day, when the bottom can't hold any longer, when the facade wears thin, when the tall and strong man's legs say 'take a seat', when our inner emptiness runs out of the thin disguises, when we've forgotten how to look to each other, then we'll buckle under! We'll fuck just about anything no matter what diseases are lurking about, waiting to kill us. We'll just go to town, go mad for what appears to be no reason at all! They made us forget that in having the strength to acknowledge our weaknesses, we have an even greater source of power.

I nearly fell in love again tonight. It makes me feel so alive. And here I am in bed, alone, writing a true story for you to read. I am happy. For the first time in my life, I feel completely connected.

A CONVERSATION WITH MY FATHER

In certain religious circles I would probably start this by saying, 'Our father who art in heaven.' But then again, Daddy, I'm lying on my stomach now, on my bed. I'm not in a church, synagogue, mosque or some religious shrine in some remote part of India. If this were twenty, thirty, forty years ago – hell if this were yesterday – and you hadn't married the woman you married, I would have slaughtered a goat now, or a chicken, spilled the blood to feed you as a sign of respect. I would have sprinkled some snuff. Only after this would I have spoken to you. Even then I would only have spoken through an elder in the family. Not directly. But this is now and the woman you married is beautiful all around. So how are you, Daddy? You took off and left me at age twelve. You were thirty-six.

I remember your tobacco-tasting kisses. I remember you rubbing my head with your big hand and saying, 'You've grown to be a big boy, huh?' I remember how dark you were. How beautiful and tall. I remember your hiss-like laughter. I remember the beauty of your smile. I guess if you hadn't given your car to your friend to drive ... I guess if your car had not gotten involved in an accident ... I guess if you didn't have a car ... you would have been stabbed to death, ridden over by a bus, or died of some natural cause or other. Is it not true that life and death are meant to happen when they choose, despite us? After all, didn't Albert Camus choose to travel by car after being told by a clairvoyant that the train was not safe, only to die when his car crashed into that very train?

I thought of you a lot after you died. I had dreams of dogs swallowing cats only for the cats to emerge from the dogs' behinds whole again, and alive. I thought you were coming back, daddy. I reacted so late. At your funeral I did not cry like the adults did. I did not cry at all. Instead, I stood there, confused. But I remember distinctly one episode when Uncle Pat sent me into this room to give mother some strength. I walked in, like a strong man, sat next to mother, and just broke down and sobbed, feeling like half a man. Oh Daddy, she just looked so fragile among all those women dressed in black. I couldn't cope. But when this confusion cleared, months later, I realized you were gone and I started having these dreams in boarding school. Oh, how I wanted you back in those days. I know that with you it was the city and that with mother it was the country for us kids. I know mother was right. So I know that in some macabre way your death freed mother to take us to her beloved countryside. I know that this move insured that none of us four boys would become criminals. But I also know how much like an angel you were, Daddy, and I love you more for the flaws. They made you so human – an angel with flaws. That's who you are to me.

Oh Dad, I could carry on until I'm blue in the face, which is possible seeing as I'm so light-skinned compared to you. You know, if there's anything that I've wanted that I can't get, it is to be as tall as I remember you to be, which is about half a head taller than me. Suffice to say that after all these years I just wanted to touch base and let you know that I love you, very much.

So long, Daddy. I hope we meet up when my turn comes.

So long.

Satire

KILL THEM ALL

Let me start by greeting everybody; boys and girls, men and women, ladies and gentlemen, the old and the young, the gorgeous and the ugly ...

God! Ugly people!!!

Anyway, let me greet the skinny ones and the ...

Jesus! Don't you hate fat people? I mean they limit your sex positions. Come on, would you let a ten-year-old elephant man or woman ride you? Would you? Huh? Fat people! They make you spend too much on petrol! They dent your car's undercarriage! Have you heard how they scrape your door every time they get off near a curb after bumming a lift?

Whoa! Wait, fatty! Wait! Let me move four metres from the pavement before you get off. Please, fatty! Please, man!

God! Fat people! You can't keep your fridge full for longer than an hour with the fat ones around! It doesn't matter about heart failure. It doesn't matter about adding more layers of fat on top of more layers of fat! They just have to eat! And so they have ridges! God! Do they have to have ridges! I mean, it would be okay if they were round, like a ball. But no! They have to look like a number of balls stuck together! And then take up the whole back seat! I think we should kill them all. And when they fall! God! Talk about earthquake creation! Imagine a fat bastard landing on you as he or she falls. Imagine a fat landing on your ass!

Nooooo!!!

You are gonna get squashed baby!!! Get out of the way!!! The fat landing's in the zone!!! Fat alert! Fat alert! Fat alert! Fat alert!

You are gonna get squashed, baby!!!!!

Don't you hate fat people? Imagine trying to design a pair of shorts that would flatter a fat person's leg (thunder legs, I might add, elephant legs, tree stump legs, fat legs). God! I think we should kill them all. Let's kill all fat people.

Just like black people!

Don't you hate blacks? I mean, you can't see them in the dark! And if they smiled to give you an indication as to where they were standing, you'd swear some sharks had mutated and gone to live on land! Blacks! Jesus! Black males! Jesus! They think their penises are Godly so they pee in the street lest we forget the myth about black men and their big dicks! And you'd think their female partners would be the most sexually satisfied of all the world's female species, would you not? But you would be wrong, would you not? Their motto is simple, isn't it? *I'm a Big Dickman,* so I don't have to work it, they say. And what about their obsession with white women?! God! Anything to look more visible in the dark! Except, of course, when they have to kill people! And that they do, don't they? Everywhere! On the farms! In the suburbs! Everywhere! They kill old people! They kill young people! They kill white people! They kill black people! They kill men. They kill women and rape them! They even kill cats and dogs, for heaven's sake! And they have such big noses! I mean, with the world's population explosion, surely we are going to run out of oxygen soon with these big noses, are we not?

I think we should kill them all.

I mean, they can't stand up individually for what they believe in so they braai each other in mobs! And they still call white people 'Baas', for God's sake! They think AIDS is a white trick to stop them from multiplying. So they are the ones dying by the millions because of this disease. The younger the black the more likely she's going to have sex without a condom! The younger the black, the more likely he's going to rape a black girl without a condom! God! They even believe they can be cured of AIDS by sleeping with babies! Then they rave on about having several girlfriends that they beat up at regular intervals. And there are so many of them! Everywhere you look is just black people!

Black people! Black people! Black people! Black people! Everywhere! Just black people! Look around you! God! They are everywhere!!!!

I think we should kill them all. AIDS has started the job. Apartheid's done half the serious preparation needed – they hate each other and all things black, so it should be really easy to set black on black deathly violence alight.

Let's kill them all. Come, let's kill the kaffirs. Come on. Let's kill them all. Let's kill the bloody blacks. Come on. Let's do it. Let's kill the blacks. Let's kill them all. They'll thank us for killing them. They are the poorest, the least educated, the most likely to steal. They have so many problems, for God's sake! Let's do it. Let's kill them all.

Just like the Afrikaners. Don't Afrikaners drive you up the wall? Don't they drive you mad with that horrible English accent of theirs? How about their psychological make-up? Isn't that disgusting? I mean, when they get depressed they shoot their babies and spouses. And they don't even know where they come from or who they are any more. The Dutch went, 'What! With your apartheid! Up yours, china! Fuck you, we are not related!' That's why you find those Afrikaners trying to be English. Just listen to how they say something like this: 'I don't know about Koos but Kobus reckons that Koos Kombuis is quite quintessential to the Afrikaner psychological make-up. But Kotie reckons fuck Kobus and Koos Kombuis, and I concur. She lives down the road in Kommissarie Straat, you know. I'm going there for tea today. She's my sister. I'm also a Koekemoer.' With every K pronounced like the 'cho' in psychology to try and sound English. Damn! Don't you hate Afrikaners? They call people *soutpiele* and then try to become those very people they call *soutpiele*. The only good thing about them is all those cats they call kaffir katties. That's a nice kick for the black hate which we need to generate to get the Black Death going. That, and the Afrikaner's hunger for the death of blacks who, we agree, have to go, is all that Afrikaners have got going for themselves.

I think we should kill all Afrikaners after they've killed the blacks. Let's kill them all. I think we should kill them all.

It's not like their fat red noses are doing them any favours in the beautiful people stakes either, for God's sake! I mean, can you point to an uglier bunch of people (excluding the Aborigines)? Can you see Terreblanche winning the Mr South Africa title this week? Can you see anybody but a confused coloured person dying to marry a de Klerk?

I think we should kill all Afrikaners! Let's kill them all. Can you imagine what a wonderful world it would be without sounds like, '*Aga nee potpiel, hoe kan jy my nie naai nie? Jy's my jong sussie!*'

I think we should kill them all! *Dead*! Kill them all. And kill those Aborigines, too, while we are at it. The Australians have done most of them in so that should take a short time to do. And then we can jump on to the business of finishing off the Aussies. Kill them all, too, is what we should do to the Australians.

Just like celibate people. God! I hate people who hate sex. Don't you? God! You watch them walking around with their thighs clutched so tight you just want to holler, '*Loosen up!*' And the gay versions of this phenomenon! God damn it! They walk about with their anuses pulled so tight you'd swear their bums were about to be pulled right into their rectums. And then you get the heterosexual males walking around with their penises tucked into their thighs and squeezed so hard you want to call them Father Something Something in some monastery. Poor penises! By the time the day ends the poor things are squashed so hard they look like snakelike pancakes! Then, of course, you get the female celibates! These walk around with their vaginas squeezed so hard and tight they look like they have knockknees. God! I hate people who hate sex! I think we should kill them all. Kill the bastards.

Kill all knockkneed people while you're at it. I mean, we all know how God wanted our legs to be and it definitely wasn't knockkneed! It isn't bow-legged either, for God's sake, or one leg shorter than the other! I think we should kill all cripples. I mean, who says people with saliva dribbling down their mouths should live? All those people in wheel chairs going on about rights! Why don't we kill them all. It would give them an early chance to come back as strong human beings with properly functioning limbs, wouldn't it? That way, we would have less people fighting for the right to be treated as human beings when they know they are half human ... because that's what bow-legged-wheel-chair-bound-knock-kneed-funny-handed-neck-askew-saliva-dribbling-brain-dead-paraplegic-quadraplegics are: half human. God, I hate cripples. Let's kill all cripples. Let's kill them all.

Let's kill all cripples. I mean imagine the toilet space we would save! Imagine all that money we would save by not building wheelchair ramps! We could use that money to fund the killing of Afrikaners! Let's do it. Let's kill all cripples. I mean, have you seen them try to run? They even call the event the something something Olympics!

The Olympics are for fully limb-functional human beings, you ...

Somebody tell them, for God's sake! No. Don't. We'll just kill the bastards. That's it. Let's kill them all. That's what I say. Let's kill the cripples. Let's kill them all.

And then you get all those beautiful people! God! Don't they just make you sick with envy? Don't they make you want to just kill something with their fucking perfect bodies and skinny looks, prancing around with their six-packs and *not fucking you back*! God! Beautiful people! Just because everybody cannot but keep asking how they got this part or that part of their body so perfect and whether or not it was really natural and how everybody keeps saying how amazing this about them is and how lovely that about them is, they think they can just lie there in bed and you must work and work and work and work ...

God! I hate beautiful people with their self-obsessed, gym-going, *everything about me is as perfect as my ass, my nose, my hair, my chest, my mouth, my bloody six-pack and my anorexia, my bulimia, my this, my that, my ... Fuuuuuck!* I hate beautiful people. I think we should kill them all. One fucking beautiful person by one fucking beautiful person they must go. I think we should kill them all. Let's kill all beautiful people. Let's kill them all.

Just like those idiots I like to call green people. Don't green people remind you of that slimy green stuff that grows on wet, rotting pipes? They are so conscious of *issues* they'd eat mouldy bread because it's *green*! They won't drink tap water because everybody everywhere is dying of the fluoride in it! I mean, *hello*?? *Fluoride?!* What a cause to take up! They won't eat meat because they'd rather go directly in competition with cows for green food. And they are so uptight. God! They are so uptight their asses are squeezed harder together than the

95

gay celibate guys! Nothing's ever green enough for these people. I think we should kill all green people. I think we should kill them all.

Let's kill all sex-loving, nymphomaniac, sex-addict freaks too, please, while we're at it. When they are females they are constantly wiping the dribble down their thighs. You allow them to sit on your leather couch and they leave a dribble patch. That's if they don't slide off it and fall, leaving a telltale, slimy-looking dribble patch behind. If they are male they can never concentrate when you talk to the horny bastards because every time a skirt walks by they get lost in imagining the dribble between her thighs and before you know it their dicks have lifted the coffee table and you've got tea all over your Sunday outfit! God! If I hate people who *hate* sex, I hate people who *love* sex even more. I think we should kill them all. And the bastards are spreading HIV/AIDS as we speak because when the dribble rolls down those thighs and that sticky goo comes out of that penis they don't think about anything except mixing the dribble with that sticky goo wherever the sex-loving nymphomaniac sex addict freaks might be at the time! And how can they even think of using a condom under those circumstances? I think we should kill them all. I mean, think of all the breeding that follows! All those unwanted babies who end up unloved, uncared for and whining and screaming and raping and stealing and looking for the love they did not get because their parents were vagina-dribble, penis-goo led, sex-obsessed, nymphomaniac, sex-addict freaks.

God, I hate babies! While we are busy mowing down these sex freaks we might as well start with those tiny little babies that are constantly crying and pissing in their pants and crying and grabbing at everything for no reason at all and crying and throwing up all the food they hollered for in the first place then crying again and messing up the whole meaning of peace in this life with their cries.

Leave me alone you baby booming freeeeak! I think we should kill all babies. I think we should kill them all. Let's kill them all.

Kill white people, too. I mean, white people can't wait to be killed anyhow. God, they suffer! Don't white people suffer too much for you? The sun turns them red, and then cancerous. And they are just like snakes. In summer you catch them crawling out of their peeled skins. The one thing going for them is probably the amount of hate they generate. We need that hatred to finish off the people we've listed so far in this speech. Whites! God! They hate the blacks, they hate the Indians, they hate the coloureds, they hate the Jews. They almost finished off the Native Americans. They killed off the Khoi and drove slaves. They killed black people, for God's sake! But that's a good thing. Sorry about that. But I still think we should kill them all. I think we should kill all white people. But maybe we should kill them last since they are so full of hate that they can finish off the rest of our death targets pretty quickly.

I mean, we could use them to kill off the Jews, for instance. Don't you think Jews should go? I mean, they are so bigoted, aren't they? The father runs a slave-driving empire while the son joins the slave-driven liberation movement. You, my friend, a slave, are now left confused in the middle, stone in hand, not knowing whether or not to throw the stone, who to throw it at or when, because the tank ready to mow you down belongs to Hamish

Senior, and Hamish Junior is standing next to you singing a freedom song off-key at the top of his voice!

And they will not be criticized! I mean what kind of people can't take criticism? Thanks to Hitler, every time you say to a Jewish person, 'Don't be racist please,' they go, 'My grandfather's father was in the gas chamber in Dachau, you know.'

'But sir, I was not in Dachau. I am not German or German speaking. I'm just a black man saying I don't need you to piss on me today, if you don't mind.'

And they have such ugly, big noses. Uglier and bigger than the blacks and only matched in size by their cousins, the Arabs. I saw an Arab and a Jew walk simultaneously up to a wall, naked, with straight hard-ons, and break their noses instead.

I think we should kill all Jews. I think we should kill all of them.

The good news is that there aren't that many of them left. Hitler already started the job and they are scared. Let's finish them off and free all that money and use it to kill blacks, kill Afrikaners, fat people, green people ...

And kill all the Arabs, too, for fuck's sake. God! I hate Arabs. What people encourages their own to blow themselves up and then call it divine sacrifice? What's good about the Arabs except that, like you and I, they hate the Jews? I think we should help them finish off the Jews and then kill them all. Or should it be the other way around, as Jews have more fire power and hate against the Arabs? Whatever. I hate them both. God, I hate Arabs. The referee says they have a corner and *bang*, right in the middle of a soccer game, they call Ahmed to come and bring stock so they can start a little corner shop. I think we should kill all Arabs as soon as they kill all Jews. What peace we would have in the Middle East. Let's kill all Arabs and free all that oil in the Middle East, sell it and fund our death drive against the Indians.

I mean, hello, what are Indians doing on planet earth, for God's sake? Don't you *hate* the way they believe they are white when they are outside Calcutta? Talk about lack of taste. Talk about self hate! Talk about wanting to be something we already knew should have been killed five whole paragraphs back in this speech. How can you love what hates you and expect to be spared the death penalty? Even if you hate blacks? It's not going to happen! Consider this: the squalor in Bombay is not of a better class than the squalor in Sebokeng. God, Indians! And what about that curry smell they bring to the party? God! I think we should kill them all. Kill all the Indians. Don't you hate how they act as if they are not part of the racism that apartheid was when all they did was rob poor blacks daily in those stupid shops they own? As if hating blacks was not their only redemption, like fools, they denied it. God I hate Indians. I think we should kill them all.

Kill animals too. They fart whenever they want wherever they are. They call in the flies (which we should kill, too, by the way), shit wherever they want, whenever they choose, and eat all the grass, getting all those slimy green people in bad moods while they are at it. God, I hate animals. To hell with them all. All they do is keep giving green people a reason to think they are important. God forbid that they should die, they think, as if that is not precisely what the world needs. God, I hate animals. I think we should kill them all and give green people a reason to commit mass suicide. What a better world we would have if that were to happen! I think we should kill all animals. Kill two birds with one stone.

Then we must kill all SPCA workers. Damn! What's with all that animal activism, man? I hate SPCA workers. I hate them. I think we should kill them all. Every time a brother tortures an animal they rush in to interfere, acting all saintly and holier than thou, knowing full well that we want all animals dead and preferably after some serious torture. God, man! I hate SPCA workers. I hate them all. I think we should kill them all.

Let's kill thin people too. Let's kill the English. God! They are an ugly bunch! Let's kill all Afrikaners, let's kill the Chinese. What are the Japanese doing on this earth, for Christ's sake? Let's kill the snakes, let's kill the birds, and kill all the fishes. Let's dry out the sea and kill the world.

I think we should kill everything. Kill all of South Africa. Kill our mothers, too. They leave our dads to have sex with us and then pretend like it's not happening. They get beaten up by our dads and act like it's not happening and then turn us into things that beat up other people or take beatings for no reason other than that we watched them take it while smiling to the world like everything was fine. Let's kill everybody.

Kill Mandela, too, for God's sake. I mean, the guy is obviously too old. Let's rest him before he kisses another white baby. Let's do it before the guy visits Robben Island one more time, empowering those Afrikaners and making them clap each time he visits that cell as they remember their days in power. Let's kill Mandela and shut down Robben Island while we're at it. Kill Tutu, too, before he cries one more time. Will somebody tell him it doesn't matter how many times he cries, he won't be getting another Nobel Peace Prize and that the Swedes are beginning to think they made a mistake, for heaven's sake! Let's kill Tutu and let's kill Mandela. Hey, let's kill de Klerk! And doesn't he deserve special mention? I mean, the sucker is clearly demented. Anybody who just hands over power to black people deserves to die. I think we should kill de Klerk as a preliminary to killing all the Afrikaners.

Kill all those coloureds while we're at it. Talk about a people with a multiple-personality disorder! One minute they are looking in the mirror and there stands Jan van Riebeeck, and then they look again and, God, it's Mazibuko! Talk about a confused bunch. The only thing going for them is their hatred for blacks. I think we should arm all coloured people, especially the pitch black coloureds, and then train them to shoot anything black. Let's arm all coloured people, especially the ones who belong to PAGAD and the gangs. Once they've done finishing each other off we can sit back and applaud before we kill all the Germans.

What have Germans got going for them except that they cut down the number of Jews? What have Germans got except that they wiped out some gays, who we have also agreed have got to go. What have Germans got, huh? For one thing, they are increasing the number of coloureds who, we do agree, must go, with their love for black people, who we have also agreed, must go, too. Germans! Just because they wiped out the Jews they must now overcompensate by sleeping with all the blacks every time they come to Africa. With Hitler gone, really, what have the Germans got?

Nothing ...

... tastes like a dead German. I think we should murder them all. I think we should kill all the Germans. Let's kill them all. Let's murder the Germans.

And what about ugly people? My goodness! Don't they freak you out? You are having a peaceful sleep and a wonderful dream, next thing, *wham*, Jonas is in the dream turning it into a nightmare. *Aaaaaahh!!!* Get the hell out, you ugly bastard! Get out of my dream! Nooooo!!!! Don't kiss me. Don't kiss me. Nooooo!!! You ugly bastard, Nooooo!!! Keep your ugly lips away!!!!

Don't you hate ugly people? What could possibly be worse to watch than two perfectly ugly people leaning towards each other to kiss at a fancy restaurant? *Ooops!* There goes your appetite. What could be worse than two ugly people kissing the air around their ears pretending to be two, beautiful, frog-leg-eating people from France at a fancy restaurant? How puke-like! Ugly people! I think we should kill them all. I think we should kill all ugly people. And yes, just like beauty, ugliness is in the eye of the beholder so you can pick your own ugly people and kill them all. You be the judge, the jury and the executioner. Let's kill all ugly people. Let's kill them all.

And then, of course, there are the sheep-shagging Australians, and the chauvinistic French pretending to be masters of love and the funny-eyed Chinese and the bloody spear-wielding Zulus and the big dick Shangaans. Will somebody tell me what the bloody Nigerians are good for on this planet?! I think we should kill all these people. I think we should kill then all.

Just like the bloody mosquitoes with their tiny bloody

voices buzzing all bloody night and stinging you like there's no tomorrow. I bloody hate mosquitoes with their malaria-wielding whiny voices and little stings. I think we should bloody well kill them all and then follow that up with fly genocide. Bloody flies, man! Spitting on my food and shitting on it then vomitting on it then eating it all up again and then vomitting again on my food, man, then shitting ... again!!! Flies must die, I swear. I think we should kill them all.

Kill everything on earth, man. Just kill, kill, kill, kill, kill, kill, kill, kill, kill. Kill them all, man. Kill. Let's roll up our sleeves and kill the world.

Kicking live at Kippie's

Good evening, ladies and gentlemen, welcome to The Black Sun ...

Sorry, we've got to start that again. How stupid. Okay, here we go ...

Good evening, ladies and gentlemen, welcome to The Victorian Toilet! No, no, it's true. You, ladies and gentlemen, are sitting inside a Victorian toilet!

You know, I can almost imagine the whole scenario. I can almost see the office where the Victorian toilet idea was hatched. They got the name first. The lefty at the corner said: 'Kippie, let's use the first name. It's easier to pronounce. People (read white people) will battle with saying Mow-way-kay-tsheee (read Moeketsi).' 'That's nice,' said the white bearded man presiding over the meeting. 'Ja, people would go to a place that Kippie owns.'

'Well ... *supposedly* owns,' said the boytjie sitting nearest to the bearded man presiding over the meeting.

'Kippie's, that's nice,' repeated the white bearded man presiding over the meeting.

'That's very nice. What about the structure?'

'Well, what about it?' said the boytjie farthest from the white bearded man presiding over the meeting of lefties.

'What should we build for Kippie?' said the white bearded man presiding over the meeting, a little irritated.

They thought about this for a very long time. It took weeks. This was very important. What should the structure be?

And one day, they are sitting in the office pondering this, and one of the publicity people goes: *'I've got it. I've got it*!'

You could hear, *Eureka*! echoing against the walls.

'A *toilet*!'

'Yeah? But isn't that a bit small?' said the white bearded man presiding over the meeting yet again.

'Why don't we make it a Victorian toilet?' exclaimed the lefty in the corner.

'My thoughts exactly.'

There were smiles all round because a Victorian toilet is indeed big.

'That's nice, very nice,' repeated the white bearded man presiding over the meeting yet again, satisfied.

And so it came to be and there, ladies and gentlemen, that's why I said, Welcome to The Victorian Toilet. It is where you are.

I'd like to thank all the people who were involved in this difficult task. I mean, say they hadn't built this toilet, where would I be performing tonight? I mean, what place would be more perfect to hold a happy seventy-sixth birthday bash for our beloved devotee Mr Mandela than right bang inside a Victorian toilet named after a great jazz musician?

Okay. Enough about that. Let's talk about black dicks. It's more fun, right? Tell me this: Why do black people pee in the streets even when they're sober? White guys here would say they are show-offs, right? Fuck that, I reckon they think we are still in the Shaka Zulu era. You know, in Shaka's time you went into the bush and squatted. When you were done, you used a leaf and left the pile for the ants and flies. I reckon black guys are backwards. Nobody pees in the streets today. You have to be mad or stuck in time to do that! These guys probably don't even know what a toilet looks like. Talk about a changing South Africa. Anyway, maybe things are changing.

You see, Rastas don't find it that easy to fuck white women any more. In previous years all they had to do was tell the potential fuck she was racist, no wonder she wouldn't fuck a black guy. The funny thing is most of the time they were right. So they struck a chord there, and you had a lot of guilt appeasement via the black dick. Amazing what black dicks can do besides urinating in the streets, right? And somebody tells you that men and women are equal! Show me one vagina that did what black Rasta dicks did in Yeoville: provide guilt appeasement for racism? What a gift to white womankind! Rasta boys, I think you did a marvelous job. I wonder why they gave Tutu the Nobel Peace Prize. You should have won it.

As you can see we are in a changing South Africa. A South Africa that needs different tactics for getting laid, thanks to Rastas and maybe to some degree Mandela and FW. Thank you guys for complicating Rasta lives in Yeoville. What a time to choose! I was just learning to make white girls guilty and you fucken change the rules! Thank you.

You can tell I'm pissed off, hey guys? It's true, I am. All I want in life is to fuck a white woman. That's all I have ever wanted. That's all black people have ever wanted. Afrikaans! No man! June 16, 1976 was about black men struggling for the right to sleep with white women. And here I was, just about getting it right and what do you know, it'll probably take Rastas another ten years to devise another system that I can adopt. Jesus, I'm pissed off! I have to wait ten years to get my first white woman. Ten years. And all it takes for white guys to fuck black women is a trip to Hillbrow and an extra fifty bucks to spare! Under apartheid I was perfecting the guilt-driven sexual home run across the colour barrier and then they released Mandela and the white girls were like, 'Guilty! For what? You have your Mandela. I'll keep my pussy, thanks.'

Mandela must promulgate a law that says: *To qualify to be citizens of Azania, white males must make a daughter each and hand them over at sixteen to Rasta social scientists who will then quickly devise another trick to get sex across the colour line now that guilt doesn't work any more.*

Okay guys, let me not burden you with my personal problems, right? But tell me something else, then. Why do South African men always say, 'Your dress is lovely,' when what they mean is, 'Please dear, fuck my brains out.' I even heard a guy talk about the tip of Kilimanjaro when what he obviously meant was the tip of his penis. I couldn't believe it! I think we are an extremely deceitful nation. I can't wait for a time when we would be truly free. When a man can walk into the Kippie's and say to Marieta, 'Let's make a baby, dear.' And she can say, 'What about the people?' And he can say, 'But they are all concentrating on jazz, lovey. Look, when they take their minds off the jazz, they concentrate on their drinks! Come. Let's do it while they take a sip.' And you can put your glass down and turn around to hear the man saying, 'Now don't scream lovey, you don't want to sell sexual shares to all these men, do you? You don't want to be on the sexual stock exchange now, ja? And she'd be going, 'Mmm, mmm, mmm, mmm.' Battling to keep herself out of the sexual stock exchange.

Let's have some honesty here. All you men here are sexist pigs, aren't you? How many of you wouldn't give your dicks away to get laid right inside Okay Bazaars? The answer is 'very few'. But the question remains: how would you do it without your genitals, huh?

You obviously think I'm preoccupied with sex. You're right. We have something in common. And you think I prefer skinny women, ja? Well let's talk about what you think is my preference, then. I love it when skinny women walk. You just hear their thin legs whistling as they cut through the air. I always enjoyed Zola Budd the most when she overtook a challenger with those skinny legs whistling at fever pitch! Isn't it amazing? Legs that sing. You can put your arms around a skinny woman and scratch your back. That would be about four days before she dies of anorexia, of course.

Forget women. My greatest love, believe it or not, is macho men. Everything is so simple for macho men. Women belong in the kitchen and they don't argue. You burp out loud and laugh at your own jokes. Then you fart and kill a few flies. You watch TV and pass out on the couch, snore and dream about kicking the ball like Naas before the madam brings you supper. It's a lovely life, because so long as you're macho, you'll be the best at fucking secretaries as long as you bring chocolate every time you come back from a business lunch. I love macho men.

I also enjoy the free spirits at The Harbour Café in Rocky Street in Yeoville, funny enough. They dress up in smelly torn jeans for show. You know, a bum sticking out here and there and then they grow their hair long you know, like flower children. They have the occasional bath on Sunday to avoid church and demonstrate their rebellion against the Christian institution. I love them. They are just like Soweto Americans. South Africans are everything but South African. They stink to feel like the flower children, they drug themselves in the hope that they'll sing like Jim Morrison. Then they wear ugly shirts, like twenty of them in the same style and then call themselves Italians. But when you ask them about spaghetti they say, 'I think it's, eh, it's a shirt designer or something. I don't know.' South Africans are wonderful people – fucked up wonderful.

But when will we be proud of ourselves? For the moment we are as bad as fat people who act skinny all their lives. Meanwhile, somebody has to keep diving under us to save us every time we fall short of other nations. That's why I prefer Zimbabweans: 'Hey, Mugabe is a fuck-up, but he's *my* fuck-up. I'll vote him in again because he's a Zimbabwean and I'm a Zimbabwean. When he fucks up some more I'll run to South Africa and fuck a lot because I'll tell them I'm a Zimbabwean citizen with a Zimbabwean leader in Zimbabwe.'

Now, *there's* a man who's proud of his roots.
Let's get it together guys, huh?
Cheers.

TWISTED AND VILE

I know and you know that in this country we never swear.
You know, somebody says 'I forgot the "fucking" car keys'
and we all zoom in on 'fucking' and forget that without
the car keys we cannot get to The Potpourri Festival.
Who knows? Maybe we just love fucking. Maybe we're
a country of romantics, which could mean we're quite
backward. You see, Romanticism is quite an old notion.
It's like living in Wordsworth's time. And that's a long
time ago. But that's obviously one side of the story, and
some would find it twisted, if not vile.

Anyway, how's this for romance in the nineties? You
walk up to a woman who for all obvious reasons is
'happily married' and ask her, 'How's your husband?'
'Oh,' she says. 'He's a comforting irritation.'

Did you ever walk up to a Zimbabwean and ask
him what he thought of Zimbabwe as a country and he
answered by saying, 'Zimbabwe has a top leader, a top
leader who is not intelligent at all.'

I went up to a guy once and asked him what he
thought of FW – de Klerk that is, not FuckWit. Now
FW is the guy who released Mandela or, rather, the
guy who happened to be in power when Mandela
happened to release himself. He's the guy who got the Wit
Wolwe so worked up they started bombing taxi ranks.
He got this place so fucked up we inherited tribal warfare
before its architects died with it. Now FW is the guy
who's got us swimming in something akin to excretion,

right? So I ask this guy, 'What do you think of our FW?' And he says to me, 'Considering that his head doesn't shine so much under the press-conference spotlight, I think his bald head's rather cute.'

You know, I wore a T-shirt with *Viva Mandela* written on it to work once and one of the drivers came up to me and said in Zulu, 'Sorry bra, but I really didn't know that *Viva* was Mandela's first name.' How's that, hey? The guy probably didn't even know whether Mandela was related to Stompie or not. For those who cannot read (and I'm sure there are plenty in this country) Stompie is the stub that was put out in an ashtray placed a little too close to our version of the Queen Mother ... Tante Elize aside, of course. Stompie is the lad who's got witnesses going, 'Winnie beat us up.' While Mandela walks besides her in this ... er ... another trial after the fact, another tragedy without the spice of Shakespearean wit and intelligence.

It's a great country, this. Don't you think? In fact if you come to Jo'burg, you can get anything you want. You want your finger chopped off? Just wear a diamond ring and step into an elevator with a few South Africans. They'll chop it off for you. You want to get buried in little pieces? Just walk up to an Inkatha supporter and say, 'I think Gatsha stinks to high heaven,' and you'll be chopped up, exactly the way you want. South Africa is a great country ... for masochists.

In fact, if we took time to film South African day-to-day events, we would probably stop the British from killing their babies slowly to satisfy the kinky sexual needs of the rich. We would make so much money in the international porn market that we would be able to lift our middle fingers to striking miners, the sanctions campaign and

Archbishop Tutu all at once. And that's only on day-to-day events. South Africa is a rich country.

This is the kind of scene God witnesses when he switches his attention to us whenever we manage to take his eyes off the red light district in Amsterdam (you must understand that he is fascinated by what goes on there, too). He sees a South African walking down a South African street. The South African checks this dude pissing against a pole in broad daylight and says to him, *Heit, my bra*. The pissing dude then turns around, waves his dick at his fellow South African and says, *Heit, my ma se kind, ek sê hoezit*? God sees a free country, a country where you can pee and shake your penis wherever you want, except outside Lichtenburg, where you get killed for peeing behind a tree a few kilometres from the town centre. God sees a confused country. He sees a coloured family trying to move into Ventersdorp and sees the white potential neighbours nicely sending their nice kids to go tell the coloured family nicely that they don't want kaffirs in their neighbourhood. God sees a polite country.

Now how do you measure the good side of politeness? If you asked a connection of mine named Karen, this would be your answer: Bake a cake with the normal cake ingredients except that instead of sugar, employ the willing services of salt. When it's done, invite a number of people over and observe those who eat the cake with smiles glued to their faces. 'How's your cake, Dave?'

'Mmm ... quite tasty, different ...'

'Do you want another piece, Dave?'

'Huh?'

'Do you want ...'

'No, thanks. No. It's lovely, though. Okay. Yes. I'll have another piece.'

How many more families are gearing kids up for this kind of experimental abuse? It's almost like the army top-class graduate who says to you: 'The general taught us, and rightly so, that in life there are things worse than death. Such as dishonour and defeat.' The man would rather insist on playing the seventy-six millionth game of backgammon rather than accept that seventy million nine hundred and ninety-nine thousand nine hundred and ninety nine games to zero might mean that the other person is better at the game than he is.

I love this place, and I truly believe that God also listens to 702 ... and that one day he heard this woman telling that hunk of a balding man John Berks that, 'I would love blacks to move into Sandton, so long as they live by Sandton standards.' Now I don't know what God's reaction to that was, but personally I would love to move into Sandton. You see, I love laser beams, and if they help lock out rapists and sadists who've run short of willing masochists, all the better. It's just those walls. They are such time wasting devices.

Check this out. Two boys get born next door to each other on the same day, right? Then they meet, finally, twenty-four years later.

'Howzit?'

'Hi.'

'Do you wanna fuck?'

'Yeah, sure, I mean, you mean, now?'

What a waste of time. Twenty-four years it takes them to get it up in Sandton.

I mean how's this country and its maids, huh? You see, at home, we always had a maid, always. My mum insisted that we call each one of them ... FW. No, I mean fuckwit or not, we had to call them 'auntie'. She said that when we could afford paying wages we could tell people what to do. So the maids at home acted as surrogate mums. They would make sure we did the dishes after meals, and we folded our blankets off the floor each morning when we got up. Now, in Sandton they have a pretty similar system. They get a maid who is normally as old as the parents or just younger if not much older. The kids call her by name and tell her what to do. It's called 'making her part of the family'. She works for the three year old. I wonder about those maids. I mean, they are pretty huge people. They have bums this big, and boobs to breast-feed Africa! Now imagine such a massive person running around a fourteen year old. Cleaning the ring after she's had a bath, picking up the towel, washing her panties at the wrong time of the month ... all of this after washing her nappies for a while. And all you hear is, 'Betty is wonderful, the kids adore her.'

'You mean the maid.'

'Yes. But in this house we call them by name. Isn't it, Betty?'

'Yes, madam.'

'Please change Linda's napkin, will you?'

'Yes, madam.'

God sees all of this. And you know what, if the fucker's got eyes he also sees Soweto.

Now enough weather forecasts have emphasized the autonomy of Soweto: *And the temperature in downtown Jo'burg, the barometer seems fixed on twenty degrees ... and it's twenty degrees in Soweto.* Soweto is independent. No questions asked.

There was a time in Soweto when a guy would come

113

up to you and say, '*Ek soek daai cherrie van jou.*' You say no, he shoots you, takes the girl and collects a few more for a week-long sexual party with his buddies.

Those were trying times, ladies and gentlemen. They demanded *ingenuity*.

So this one girl agreed to everything, stripped down naked, spread her legs wide open and said to the leader of the pack, 'My witchdoctor worked on me. The first boy dies, but the rest of you can sleep with me for as long as you want. So come taste the sweet cake.'

Do you see democracy working in a country with a history like that? You know, I can almost understand the frustration of being a teacher in South Africa today. Imagine having to hold a general election for students to determine what should go into the maths textbook! And then following that up with a by-election in class to determine the answer to one plus one. Can you top that for the definition of *hell*? Pass one pass all. As though all blacks share Steve Biko's IQ.

But maybe teachers can take heart in that maybe what they really mean by democracy is that when a child says one plus one equals three he or she shouldn't be tortured. Imagine if you asked why and she said, 'It's three, sir, because when two people work together well, it produces a third person who is invisible, but helps make the workload much easier to carry for the two involved.' Imagine again if you asked and he said the answer's one and a half, ma'am, because when my parents get together they get a baby.

That reminds me of the three-year-old only child who overheard gasps and moans from her parents' bedroom. Out of curiosity she leaned a little closer and heard her mother say: 'Oh baby, oh my sweet baby, I love you baby, give me more, more, more baby, oh my sweet baby. I love you baby.' The next day the only child walked up to the mother and said, 'Mummy, how many babies have you got?' And you thought that they were nitwits with no brains. You thought, they can be molested and it won't even show. Or are you generally uncaring people?

Why are so many adults falling in lust with three year olds?

'You know bra, there's this chick I know. She's got straight honey blonde hair, a cute rosy bum and fuckall hair on her body. Fuckall hair, bra, and she doesn't even have to shave. Hey, I dig chicks with fuckall hair on their bodies. But her mother watches her like a hawk. I can't even get a second alone with her. Imagine if I had two to myself. My three-year-old daughter. Hey, you reckon at three they know fuckall! You must check my daughter, bra, she's game. Imagine if I had two. Imagine if I could fuck openly like I wanna fuck. Not like my dad used to fuck me. Always in the dark. Always when everybody was out. Hey, I hated the secrecy. Imagine if I could fuck openly like I wanna fuck? Who the fuck you calling a paedophile? Who the fuck you fucken calling a paedophile? I wanna fuck who I wanna fuck when I wanna fuck. I wanna be free in this country too, bra. Who the fuck you fucken calling a paedophile?'

Any feminists in the house? Okay, I know, in this country you don't move from one touchy subject straight onto another. So let's talk about vegetarians. I know. You're going to tell me that vegetarianism is about not eating dead meat, dead food. I just don't feel like arguing about the scientific point at which a vegetable or any organism dies, otherwise we might find ourselves announcing something like this over the radio: 'Four vegetables died in Soweto today, three of them very seriously.'

I don't know. Sometimes I just wonder, though. What is feminism? Is it growing your hair long like Koos De Walt Groenewald? Is it leaving your teeth to brown like Khazamula Mlangeni's? Is it dressing down and chewing gum and stinking like a sewer for months on end? Is it becoming a man? Do you have to stink to teach about feminism? You see I'm from the old school. I like to believe that a bad smell stays a bad smell even among well meaning people. You see, somebody farts, right, but they let off a really bad one. The question then becomes, Who farted? Why would they do such a thing? Who is sitting closest to the person who farted? As you can see, the questions quickly evolve onto scientific aspects of diffusion.

You will have noted also that none of the questions posed by a bad smell include, 'Are you a Muslim? Do you live by traditional African standards? Are you a peasant Israeli Jew?' Questions which immediately tell you whether or not the man still has his foreskin, whether the woman's clitoris has been chopped off. Ouch! Aah, you didn't think Jews and Muslims had anything in common, did you? Especially with the Gulf crisis. Well, maybe they, together with traditionally bound Africans, share a conspiracy against womankind. You see, remove a man's foreskin, enhance his sexual gratification. Take off a woman's clitoris and you do the exact opposite. Simple, isn't it? I don't know. I just think that bad smells are non-sexist because they are essentially sexless. I just wonder if we need to smell bad to teach sexists about feminism.

I remember this Yeoville party once. I was dancing when I felt this vigorous jab between my ribs. I turned around and came face to face with this woman. She said, 'Look where you're dancing, prick.' I looked at her and leaned over and said, 'Feminism's good for you. You can be real butch like a man and then fuck all men over.' She didn't bother me after that but I can assure you, I will not allow any daughter of mine to go out with a girl like that. She can choose any girl to fuck with, but not that. Not scum like that.

Right now I'd like us to gather together, in a non-sexist fashion, and find Salman Rushdie and kill the mother-fucker! I mean the guy wrote *The Satanic Verses,* for Allah's sake! What has he got up next? What if he started screaming, 'Let all non-Muslim, non-virgin women marry in as good a marriage ceremony as all Muslim virgin women.' What if he knelt in the middle of an Iranian street and pleaded, 'Please Allah, don't let a single Muslim country chop off a single woman's clitoris.' That would be a menace! Let's find Salman, kill him, take the bounty on his head and donate it to The Foundation For The Preservation Of Traditional Methods Of Perception.

Song: *I want to go to heaven and be with Jesus*

Now. let's take a look at the people under the guiding light of Jesus Christ their saviour, Amen.

Song: *I know the Lord will make a way for me ...*

I personally believe that they are blind by now. You see, Jesus shines with such an intensity that there could never be another possible physical manner of adjustment. Jimmy Swaggart, that stalwart of the Christian faith, that genius of a preacher, the man you didn't have to travel to listen to, the man who would come to you right in your own living room and give you deliverance from that vile thing code-named 'sin'. Jimmy (now I can call him by his first name, brother, he came to our house often enough in his heydays, well, I shared him with a few million other houses back then, but it was still special) got so blind under that light, he found himself waking up once, twice, three times more times, in a prostitute's abode with the heebie-geebies. He was blinded by that Christian intensity that Jesus radiates.

You are crap. You brothers and sisters are pieces of shit. You are dirty, you were born dirty and you are going to die dirty. And *yes*, praise God, you need to be dirty to be cleaned. You need to disappear to be visible and Jesus Christ in his loving spirit died to grant you life so that you may die to earn it.

Yes. That's the meaning of life. It's so slippery it's like living in a farming area. Do you know what the definition of a gigolo is in a farming area? It's my cousin, brother. You'd catch him patiently cleaning his dad's favourite pig's backside. In the later evening he would walk up to it and enjoy the glories of the heebie-geebies. A true gigolo, he loved nature long before Greenpeace.

That's the meaning of life. I believe that the reason it's so slippery is that it's so relative. Yeah, just like relativity. When Einstein was asked to define what he meant by relativity he said, 'My friend, if you sit on a burning stove for a second, it feels like a decade. But if you spend three glorious hours with a loved one, it feels like a mere second.

That's relativity.' And somebody took the very same concept and used it to commit genocide in Hiroshima.

That is the meaning of life. Even in South Africa.

Now before I go, I'd like to share your history and my history with you. You see, I grew up in Soweto. And on a typical Soweto winter's night you would do the dishes after supper, argue less with your brothers and sisters and prepare your clothes for school the next day. You know, you'd do everything the way mummy likes it. You'd then walk up to her and tentatively ask if you could go out for a while. If you were lucky, she'd say yes. You'd walk out that door and out through the gate and at a distance, you'd see a fire burning. You see, in those days we made fires and cared fuckall for the ozone layer. We burnt plastic and wood and when we got angry we burnt each other, although a little less than we do today. Around those fires is a heritage I'll hold dear to my heart for as long as I live. And that heritage is not the glue-sniffing that caught on. It isn't the little fights we shared. It is the singing, the sudden magical outburst into song. I'd like to share that heritage with you tonight. There would be a lead singer or two and they would do a piece like this:

Song: *Heela mafik'izolo ... heela u khalela 'ni*

And the rest of the circle would back the lead with a sound like this:

Song: *Dzawuwaa dzawuwaa dzawuwawuwaw dzawuwaw dzawuwaaa ...*

Now if you put the two together, this is how it would sound with one note missing

Song: *Heela mafik'izolo. Dzawuwa. Heela ukhalelani. Dzawuwaa. Heela umam'uhambile. Dzawuwaa. Ukhalalelani bo ukhalela ubani. Dzawuwa.*

About ninety per cent of the people who used to sing around those fires believed then, and still do today, that white people cannot sing. That makes me wonder about Sting's parentage, you know, Bles Bridges? I wonder what colour the Welsh are supposed to be. Anyway, I'd like us to prove that ninety per cent I talked about wrong tonight. I'll do the lead singing and you just back me up when I key you in.

Song: *Heela ...*

South Africans, what have we in our history?

We have Amahipi na Ma 'hi man'. Black men in bell-bottoms and high-heels and love and peace signs. Men who knew about Hillbrow when killing a black man was like squashing a fly to a white man. We had men, some of whom were as homosexual as any gay man in the world. We had Americans in Africa. They would twang their English and swing their bums walking down the road. 'Hey man, how're you doin'?' And we were proud!

We have Amapantsula, guys who would hit a girlfriend across the face with a brick and drag her across the street for a quick fuck.

We have Sophiatown, a dwelling area demolished by the Afrikaner to make room for more Afrikaners.

Sophiatown was bustling with life, they would tell you. *In Sophiatown het ons toppies gehad wat tsotsitaal soos jy dit nie ken gepraat het. Ons het toppies wat mbaqanga gespeel gehad. Toppies wat na ou Dizzie Gillespie op Saterdag geluister het. Mcha toppies, slim toppies. Toppies wat gin en brandy en whiskey skoon gedrink het. Jaa, Sophiatown.* We recounted with pride how a guy in Sophiatown would walk into a shebeen with his enemy's head in his hand and demand money from the shebeen queen and her customers. Today, we do it with more style. We chop off a fellow man's head and toyi-toyi around it.

The brightest sparks in black communities go on to have white girlfriends and this is applauded because it upgrades neighbourhoods. When black people get on a bus and white people refuse to sit next to them they get so angry, they just want to commit suicide! Talk about pride and dignity!

How's that, hey? This country has so much beef, we got so sick of watching it braai that we started experimenting with braaing humans. The next step is checking out what they taste like! I see that happening because we, in this country, search for solutions in history. You know, de Klerk says 'Operation iron fist' and we say 'We'll go back to arms!' Maybe the next step backwards is, 'Hey, I wonder how cannibals lived in those days? We've watched him enough now, let's taste his balls. We'll try the next one on the microwave. Jesus, human balls taste lekker, hey?' And then, what do you know? Someone will say human balls are good for fertility! If you're impotent, try human balls braaied medium to well done!

And there you have it. We're in business, making history for future textbook sales. It's just that we have so much of this history already. And maybe we build too much of the present history on the old stuff. So how can Biko be right? Can any South African man be truly on his own when we find so much to believe in history. That's why I keep singing to myself, 'They say they believe in yesterday. Please don't believe in yesterday.' I do it to try and see if I am truly on my own.

I'm afraid Biko is wrong, guys. No South African man is on his own. We have history behind us and with us.

You are as black as a Shangaan! We despise black so much that we label what we consider the worst of its kind the blackest. We aspire to being white so intensely that if the white man doesn't ban skin lighteners, we cannot stop using them. We are so willing that at any given time a white man can pay a black man to kill a black man and the dead black man's friends will simply turn around to find other black men, children and women to kill in revenge! What happens to the monies we rob from the banks? How much of it pays for university fees? But wait! Who needs school when Bantu education is still in full swing? Who needs a multiracial university when we must identify with the comrades in the townships?

Is it pride and dignity that makes us douse our own in petrol and set them alight for the whole world to see? Is it a sign of strength that we can chop up a man, light a cigarette and watch him kick a few times before he dies? We must be valiant because at twelve years old our sons and daughters can watch a black man fry another and not look away or vomit or scream. They can watch a man being stabbed by other men to death and ask how they can help, if they haven't figured it out themselves yet.

I'm afraid Biko is wrong. Black man, you are not on our own. You have a history behind you and with you.

Yes, it is a history. And a rich history at that. A history of gifted writers who swept through the fifties. Can Themba; a history of singers with voices to shut the birds; Miriam Makeba; a history of artists who even outside Azania created Azanian images that looked like they still woke up inside Azania; Gerard Sekoto; a history of thinkers in politics, in social norms, in philosophy. We have fathers in Robert Sobukwe; we have brothers in Steve Biko.

KHAZAMULA THE NERD
(An inspirational autobiography for the upliftment of all important South Africans).

Good evening, ladies and gentlemen. I am very happy that you came to the meeting tonight, my lovely comrades. What I did to prepare for this momentous occasion was to ask my half-sister Marietjie to help me prepare this speech because she writes better and because I can't write at all and because I have a short memory. In fact, what you've heard me say up until now is written down here. I'm not supposed to say this, but I believe in honest talk between White people. And I am White so it makes sense. You might be shocked by this but it is true. Just like some White people have funny shaped hands and maybe one leg shorter than the other and walk like this (*the speaker demonstrates the walk of a disabled person*). I happen to have been cursed with a darker hue. I'm not lying and this is serious so don't giggle too loudly. Thank you. I am more like a black and white picture which is backlit, you see. It is very difficult to see the colour of the subject under those lighting conditions unless of course the subject talks to you.

So there. I am a White man. I just happed to be trapped in a black skin for I don't know what reason except that God made a mistake, a big mistake. That's all I know and I'll tell you more about that. And don't forget, it is very important that you remember that this is a meeting of Die Gereformeerde Black Brothers of which I am chairman and Marietjie secretary. And that this is a speech, written down to be read so that I don't make a fool of myself. Thank you.

Well, Marietjie wrote this biographical speech because the more you learn about other people's achievements and understanding of the world, the better it is for you to understand your own life. That's what Marietjie says. So the idea was to tell you about me so that you can learn more about you from my profound knowledge and understanding of my life as profoundly understood and written by Marietjie. This is how it goes. Thank you. Er, by the way, my name is Khazamula but I prefer Charles, to be honest, which is my second name. Well, here goes my story.

I used to think I was a nerd, you know. I thought I was a nerd with real nerd toppings from pure nerd stock in nerd county: downtown Jo'burg. Nerd county, home of *Willem warmgat, my Willie*. And I'll tell you why.

We, that is our family, sort of moved into the backyard of Baas Koos Koningin, the fat one. Up to today I don't know why he was called 'Koningin' because he had a dick. I understand why he was called 'the fat one'. He had a really big one, well, that's what my mother told me.

Anyway, that's a small detail. My mother was a domestic for Baas Koos Koningin, the fat one. Then she started sneaking my dad in during the night, and they fucked. Oh my goodness! I don't believe Marietjie wrote that. I guess it is natural so we can say it. What can I say? Anyway, I remember God looking down and saying, '*You black shits! Fucking on my beloved white Koos Koningin's own backyard! I'll show you something, you fucks!*'

I was kind of shocked by that, you see. I mean, God swearing and all that! You see, I heard him because at the time I was sort of floating about heaven. You know, sort of God's one hundred billionth mistake. He had hoped to make another White to groom into another Verwoerd in South Africa. And, alas, to my peril, he dropped me in the soot, you know, where they normally drop ashes from hell. And I came out all black!

I'm not lying. God, kill me if I am.

Anyway, I was sort of floating about heaven, bored and pissed off with my colour plight when I heard him say, '*You black shits! Fucking on my …*' and I coughed. That's when he turned around and said, 'Oh! There you are Khaz, you have such a lovely skin. You are so beautiful!'

But I could see it in his face. He was lying. Please don't giggle, this is serious. God did not like those people down there and he was pissed off with my falling in the soot. So he arranged my descent into Africa before fixing my colour. I'm not lying. Really! The next thing I knew, somebody was screaming and crying and I was being forced out of some dingy hole screaming and shouting for God to fix my colour back to the white it was supposed to be. But before I knew it, before my screaming prayers could be heard in heaven, somebody was kissing my bloody body and what do you know? I opened my eyes and there I was, right inside Baas Koos Koningin's Backyard!

And I knew I was right. Please concentrate, this is serious. God sent me to curse that woman for fucking on Baas Koos Koningin's backyard! He knew that she and her man couldn't afford me or anyone else for that matter. He knew that they could barely survive on their own, let alone if they had children! But they had to be taught a lesson, so he sent four more mistakes down there and before Baas Koos knew what had hit him, there were five babies in his backyard and he got jealous. He threw my dad out and fucked my mother himself and Marietjie was born. She is a half-mistake. God said, '*You kaffir-lover shit! I'll show you something, you black ass-creeper!*'

And he sent a half-mistake down.

If you ask Marietjie, she'll tell you. She fell half into the soot before God grabbed her and pulled her to the top. She also had the good fortune of having been designed to be white. But God was angry with her for falling in the soot and because he's so busy designing cockroaches and ants and snakes and stuff like that he had no time to fix her colour, so he used her to curse Baas Koos Koningin for 'fucking a mistake'. That made her a nerd too, like me. Though I must admit, less of a nerd, really.

Anyway, Baas Koningin's backyard sort of grew bigger with more Marietjies being born every now and again. I'm not lying. Baas Koningin's wife left him together with two of the three children, Bennie and Rika. But Kobus stayed because he was now enjoying the first Marietjie's between-the-legs. I don't blame Baas Koningin's wife for leaving, though. Baas Koos was deteriorating at full speed.

At about that time the first calamity hit South Africa. The law for the White fuck White only and mistake fuck mistake only went away. Please, stop giggling, this is serious and I'm telling the truth here. That law went away, right? And that's when my mother moved into the main house. But to be honest, Baas Koos Koningin was a bit too ugly to marry another decent-looking Afrikaans wife with only a little bit black in her. So my mother moved into the main house and fucked Baas Koningin until he died of orgasmophobia. Well, that's a term that I coined to enrich our language, really. I see Marietjie likes it too. That's nice of her to use it in this speech.

Seriously, though, Baas Koningin was coming every night for every year of the last five years of his sixty-five years. He died, naked, his body pink with sexual delight. The only problem is that he got it all every morning from a mistake. I don't think he'll enter heaven. And that's how it should be.

Anyway, that is how we inherited the main house. My mother, her mistakes, that is the other four and I ...

Er, I seriously urge you not to laugh and giggle, please. I'm laying my soul down for your benefit here, you know? It is not funny, really. Anyway, like I was saying, the inheritors of the main house were my mother, her mistakes, Marietjie and the other half mistakes, nine to be exact. You know, God just got so angry with Baas Koos sometimes! I remember one day, he just sent three half-mistakes at once, just like that! Talk about angry! Anyways, the other inheritor was Kobus, of course, the one who was now enjoying the first Marietjie's between-the-legs.

And around about that time we all got invited to a struggle meeting. We said *no*! I mean we won our struggle!

Okay, fair enough, we still get the odd parcel with a dead dog and a '*kaffir gaan huis toe*' note, but hey, we won our struggle. We even have half-mistakes who will produce quarter-mistakes who will produce one-eighth-mistakes who will produce one-sixteenth-mistakes all the way until God likes us, too. I'm not lying. And if we carry on like this, God might choose our family of nerds in downtown Jo'burg to produce the next Jesus. I'm not lying and it will happen because we are dedicated and determined to be even whiter than Verwoerd!

And the Jews are out of the race. They've lost it because they go by the law Jew Fuck Jew and cling onto the Old Testament! God now thinks he made a mistake by making them the chosen race because they don't try to be more Caucasian, you know. They don't even try to improve and be more white whilst we are determined and dedicated. So it goes without saying, *we will definitely get the next Jesus as soon as the angels have the next election.*

I can tell you now, God won't choose Terreblanche because his tummy's too big and pale. And he's ugly. His wife is ugly and his child is ugly. And he doesn't know how to fuck properly. And he's like a fat bully in the school-yard. And Marietjie tells me he probably sticks boerewors up his arse to reach orgasm. Don't ask me how she found out. If I know her properly, she most likely found this out at some graveyard some time back. But worst of all, Terreblanche probably has too much black blood in him. That's one sin that God never forgives.

And he won't choose the Mandelas either! First of all they are black. Even worse, Winnie has the cheek to wear garments designed by mistakes on her black body. And she doesn't even try to disguise her colour by using skin-lighteners. What cheek! She was doing better when she appeared to be killing black stompies but then she went to court and denied it! But even worse than that, her black babies make babies with other black babies without even marrying those babies. We all know how God hates sex before marriage.

And why would God choose de Klerk? He's changed sides now. He's forgotten which side his bread is buttered! And his lungs are just about as black as some mistake's face in Soweto. Worse still, his family members fuck half-mistakes and then go so far as to get engaged to them! And his English is not poetic like mine. He speaks it like some Shangaan or Zulu chief in some bundu republic!

And why would God choose Gatsha? He won't! Reason? Obvious: he's ugly and he doesn't want to die. If it was true that his black people are killing other black people, God might choose him. But he keeps denying it, not realizing that when he dies, which might be soon, it could be his only chance to get to heaven. But he has more problems. He is married to a mistake. As a result, his babies are all mistakes! If he doesn't watch out Winnie will kill them. I tell you, she hates black stompies.

So *fuck Gatsha. Fuck de Klerk. Fuck Terreblanche, fuck …* I'm sorry. I got a little bit carried away there. But believe me, *I am as refined as the next White man.* And seriously, look to the late baas Koos Koningin's backyard babies now in the main house receiving '*kaffir gaan huis toe*' notes. We will bring the next Jesus because we only fuck White (*the speaker mock laughs out loud*). And we love Britain more than kaffir-filled Africa. Baas Koningin even found the first Marietjie a Dutch passport and we're proud of this. We can slip in and out of this kaffir-filled continent as we please.

That's why I'm not a nerd really any more. I'm a nerd with a mission and that makes a big, fat difference. In fact, whenever the Marietjies in the house get a chance, they get white injections from white boys to purify their blood. And I can tell you now: I will be a grandfather to a white nation soon. And that's on top of bringing the next Jesus. Hah, hah.

I'm a mistake with a mission and I'd like you all to sign up at the end of this meeting. Like I mentioned earlier, I am the president of an excellent group of backyard individuals. It is called Die Gereformeerde Black Brothers. And don't despair, it is non-racial although we'd prefer more whites. But that's okay. We'll make it non-racial because of the echoes of this coming new South Africa that is fucking things up for me and my kind. As soon as things settle down we'll make it exclusively white. We'll just ask people to send in their pictures and then draft letters to gracefully tell all the black applicants to, er, fuck off.

Forward met Die Gereformeerde Black Brothers Forward! Er ... this is where you all spiritedly scream, 'Forward!'

Forward met Die Gereformeerde Black Brothers Forward!

Okay, we'll get you to do it once you've signed up to join. And don't worry about the mistakes who jump on board now. We'll get rid of them in time, okay? We'll get rid of them. Don't worry about that.

Forward met Die Gereformeerde Black Brothers Forward!

Well, I guess that sort of sums up the meeting. If you have any queries please, I'm here right now for you my darlings and all those other brothers who know the right direction. But most importantly, I am here for all those brothers and sisters who are scared, and rightly so, of the onslaught of all these mistakes that fill up this, our beloved country, Suid Afrika.

So, if you want to know more about me, my mission, my background, or interesting things like whether I would have loved to have had intercourse with a detainee's wife while he was serving over twenty-five years in prison, just ask. You know, interesting questions like, 'How does it feel to be white?' You know? Do I wear white underwear? Do I promote skin-lightening lotions? Whether I'd like Michael Jackson to front and pour money into Die Gereformeerde Black Brothers. Whether I think his new nose is cute, you know. Interesting questions like, 'What do I think of movies with too many blacks in them?'

You know, you can ask about Spike Lee, that American short man who makes all those movies which only star mistakes? Whether I'd like to fuck him up his nigger arse and teach him to be a proper white and then formerly introduce him to Michael Jackson who will then introduce him to his plastic surgeon who would then fix his nigger nose. I'd also like to tell you about the operation I had to change the colour of my balls and reduce the size of my JimJack ... you know, my what's its name (*points at his penis*) so that I could be more like a real white man. Ask me about my movement forward into becoming the representative of light and all things civilized and Western. You know, like popcorn and war artillery, gay basking and paki bashing, colonization and kaffir bashing and Jew hating; the glory of conquering inferior nations and teaching them manners and obedience!

Now that you know where I'm coming from, ask me all those intelligent questions. I'm here for you, my wonderful white darlings, and I'm not excluding those mistakes who know the way to go. White is a state of mind. You, too, can be hard if you take the time to learn from me, Michael Jackson, the coloureds whose hair could not hold a pencil, and so on and so forth. Ask me now. This is that section of the meeting where you kill the panel with questions. I am the panel ... kill me. I mean with questions, that is.

Anyway, be that as it may, as Marietjie the half-mistake who is my half sister – which means she's already a quarter mistake, which means we have indeed moved farther towards our goal, as she would say – be that as it may, you have just witnessed the aura of great leadership. I know I am not Mahatma Gandhi or Biko. I'm not black. They are. I'm not Boesak or Rajbansi either; they too are black! That's the bottom line! You can't be black and make a good leader. For instance, take Mahatma Gandhi. That man's work was simply overrated if you ask me. Okay, so he starved and people made salt. He starved some more and some killings stopped. But do you know that he once took a goat to England? I mean really! He took that goat to England, right? And it farted everywhere like goats do, and burped, stinking up everything, right? He took a live goat to the middle of civilization! I mean, talk about a little man with little manners. Granted, apparently some

English women on seeing him went, 'Oh look at that cute little man! I'm sure he fucks up. I'd like to try him, at least for a change. He's so eccentric!'

So what! I can tell you now, if four English women wanted Mahatma, then a *dozen* will want me! Period. In fact, what he achieved had nothing to do with his greatness. It was simply because our brothers in England lost it for a little while. For instance, take the example of the English women wanting Gandhi. It was simply because the English boys were insisting on quickies and the missionary style where they are on top all the time! What has that got to do with Mahatma Gandhi's greatness?

Granted, when he starved, a whole nation stopped. Whereas today, a noble man like Piet Skiet starves himself, you know, quite seriously too, only to hear FW say, '*Vok-off jou poes!*' I mean, what's this country coming to? Let's just say Piet is not to be compared to mistakes, all-right? Like that Gandhi fellow. Piet Skiet's too great for that. But at the same time Piet must stop imitating the very people we so rightfully hate. Like Indians and blacks! Otherwise, he'll end up writing books such as *I Write What I Like*. Like that fellow Biko, who was as big a mistake as Gandhi.

I am determined and I will not be wavered like a tree in the wind!

Lovely line, that. You know, Marietjie can write when she wants to. I mean, this is beautiful. I will read that line again so that you can feel it's poetic power because you must be sick of those chief-like speeches by FW by now. Listen.'

133

I am determined and I will not be wavered like a tree in the wind!

How's that, huh? I love that line because it is not just poetry for poetry's sake.

I will move forward and attain my goal. My family will, through Die Gereformeerde Black Brothers, produce the next Jesus and he will be white. And God will forgive Marietjie and me for half-falling and falling in the soot ... respectively.

I will not imitate Mahatma, who fell in the soot, too. That's losing focus. Anyway, I don't think he was that great, anyhow. Now Piet Skiet, that's my idol. He must just stop imitating people. I mean, I don't even think we should be calling them people. Why is he imitating things like Biko or Mahatma? I think that's a downfall for white supremacy! In any event, times have changed. Nations don't listen to half-starved-to-death-little-men any more. My brother Piet must wake up, you know. He must look up to giants. Like Napoleon. *He* was White. And Hitler! There's a white giant. And of course Verwoerd. A man who knew blacks to the last cell. How they breathe, what they eat, where they live, how they breed, what their aspirations are, where they sleep and how. A man who even knew how blacks think. That's who Piet must look up to, *Verwoerd*.

Now people, and I mean *people* now, not those black things parading around as people and trying to rob us Whites of our very humanity to the extent of forcing us to shoot when we'd rather not! We don't want to shoot!

That's a fact! What with Greenpeace and the animal rights movement! People, we seem to be losing the meaning of powerful words, you know, powerful words like *kaffir, coolie, boesman*, powerful words, you know, like *whore*. Words that keep things in perspective. I'm worried because the communist onslaught is not over yet, I'm telling you! We will bat our eyelids and they'll simply descend upon us, rape our mothers and daughters and sisters and wives. And I hear they are catching up sexually. They also have gays these days. Our brothers and sons and fathers and husbands are not safe either. No! I repeat, no! No! let's not forget the power of words that keep things in perspective. Call a woman a bitch and watch her obey you. Especially after the I do, I do, I do in church. Go through that little ceremony. I tell you, it's nothing compared to what you can get the woman to do for you once it's all on paper.

Call a black man a *kaffir* and watch him run and hoe the fields. Isn't that what Verwoerd taught us that blacks know best? We must never forget these important lessons! I mean, what are these baldheads doing, huh? PW gives blacks the licence to. I mean, I can understand them saying, '*Swaartes, hier's 'n tractor, gaan werk op die land. Julle moet net onthou ... dis my land! Kom nou, ry julle.*' I can understand that. But to say, 'Here's my white daughter. Fuck her.' Uh-uh, that's too much. I mean, that's the trigger! A black boy fucks your daughter with that big black dick! That's it! When he leaves her she'll be running after the horses for sex! And he will. Let a black man fuck a white woman, the next day he wants to be chairman. Then he wants to run the country! And what happens to white supremacy then, huh?

I tell you, let's stop this shit. Let's stop it. Otherwise we'll go to restaurants and they'll serve us the same shit we ignored. Seriously. You'll open a bottle of wine and *whiff*, the same shit will hit your nose. And there won't be any forks. You know, blacks still eat with their hands. And I see some of us Whites have started thinking that it's quite exotic, you know. How primitive! I, Khazamula – I mean Charles – would rather jump in the sea than see us eat this shit at restaurants! They say *one settler one bullet*! Who made that bullet, huh? Who made that bullet? It was Baas Koos Koningin's ancestors. In fact, *I* made it, by inheritance. And now they want to threaten me with my invention! I'm telling you, that's what happens when a mistake fucks a White! The next thing, they'll be trying to sell helicopters and Lamborghinis to me. Already, I'm buying boerewors from blacks! I mean the name states clearly: boerewors. Who's a boer? It's Baas Koos Koningin! It is me by moving into that main house. So what are blacks doing with my boerewors?!

Really now. I hate PW. That baldheaded, slimy dickhead! He started all this with those mistake fuck White laws! I'll kill him!

Piet Skiet's men must just stop acting like mistakes. They must stop starving to death. I was very happy when they did, actually. It is not them who must die. It is PW and FW and Mandela and that kind of rubbish. Not those fine soldiers of noble beliefs! No! Never! I mean, if Marius hadn't fucked those army boys, the army would be on our side now. But, no! He had to forget White supremacy, go to the barracks, call a few boys and say, '*Laat ek jou poephol slem, ou pel*'. Who would say no to that man of high integrity?

But then he had to fail to see beyond the poephol. I would not be surprised to hear that he mixed with those skelm blacks who go about teaching our daughter to wear kikoys in those slimy places like Yeoville in Johannesburg! I wouldn't!

But you and I – and I am including those few blacks who know on which side their bread is buttered – will, through Die Gereformeerde Black Brothers, fix this shit.

Forward met die Gereformeerde Black Brothers Forward!

Er, this is where you all scream *forward*!

Forward met die Gereformeerde Black Brothers Forward!

You know, I spend time to prepare great speeches, and if people are not saying 'fuck you' under their breath, they are wishing I was dead. I feel very embarrassed, you know. It makes me remember those days when I was dying to be called up to the army, you know, before the animal rights movement had too much power and we could kill mistakes freely. I waited. You know, my fellow Whites were called up and I waited and the envelope never arrived at Baas Koos Koningin's backyard. I felt snubbed, you know, like now when I deliver great speeches. They could not see how white I am and the sun here does not help, you know. And this reminds me. Let's be proud of the colour white. Stay indoors, fellow Whites. And take it from me, there's nothing worse than being mistaken for a mistake when in fact you are lily white. Really.

And one more thing before I go away to give you time to think about my movement: this thing of dividing our rugby teams up. It's like tribalism, you know. It is not right. It seems as though by staying in this black continent we assimilate the things mistakes do. Let's have one rugby team and play friendlies. Let's leave tribalism to mistakes. After everything, we are united under one banner. We are White! And let's not forget that. Never!

You know I sit in boardrooms at White companies because that's home, right? You can't expect me to handle blacks like I knew them! It's impossible! But do you know what actually happens? I get asked constantly about how I think mistakes will like this or that. How am I supposed to know? Anyway, it's because I'm constantly mistaken for a mistake. I just hope Terreblanche takes over soon. He would understand.

I'd like you to join me in a song that epitomizes what Die Gereformeerde Black Brothers stands for. Please don't embarrass me by doing what you did when I said:

Forward met die Gereformeerde Black Brothers Forward!

You see? You are doing it again, embarrassing me with your silent stares. Anyway, I'll sing because I believe and maybe you'll come to your senses and sing too.

Song: *Siyaya in the white world. Ho siyaya in the white world. We get all the jam in the white world. Ho siyaya in the white world. Ho siyaya in the white world …*

(*Stops singing abruptly*)

You make me feel embarrassed, you. I feel like a piece of shit, really. I feel like Terreblanche when he was caught with that very pure white woman in the graveyard. I feel naked. You make me embarrassed, you know, really. And you'll burn in hell for it, really. You will. S'true because when we bring the next Jesus I'll tell him you don't believe, you atheists! God must burn you all! Really!

Other fiction titles by Jacana

O'Mandingo!
The Only Black at a Dinner Party
by Eric Miyeni

Beginnings of a Dream
by Zachariah Rapola

Coconut
by Kopano Matlwa

How We Buried Puso
by Morabo Morejele

Miss Kwa Kwa
by Stephen Simm

Six Fang Marks and a Tetanus Shot
by Richard de Nooy

Song of the Atman
by Ronnie Govender